RED HOT ICE-BREAKERS
FOR CELL CHURCHES
HOUSE GROUPS & YOUTH WORK

RED HOT ICE-BREAKERS

FOR CELL CHURCHES
HOUSE GROUPS & YOUTH WORK

MICHAEL PUFFETT

AND

SHELDON ROTTLER

MONARCH
BOOKS

First published in the UK by Monarch Books in 1999

ISBN 1 85424 456 6

Editorial office: Monarch Books,
Broadway House, The Broadway, Crowborough,
East Sussex TN6 1HQ

Unless otherwise stated, Scripture quotations are
taken from *The Holy Bible, New International Version*, copyright ©
1973, 1978, 1984 by International Bible Society. Used
by permission of Hodder & Stoughton Ltd.

British Library Cataloguing Data
A catalogue record for this book is available
from the British Library.

Designed and produced for the publisher by
Bookprint Creative Services
PO Box 827, BN21 3YJ, England.
Printed in Great Britain.

DEDICATION

To Heather, Amy and Jessica,
my precious wife and daughters.

Michael

To all my friends who so faithfully over the years
have laughed at my humour. Especially to my wife,
Andrea, and my best friend, Neil Barwood, who are
teaching me to laugh at myself. Thanks guys.

Sheldon

CONTENTS

FOREWORD

We live in a day where the advent of new testament church life is being lived out in a manner that has possibly not been observed since the Acts church.

This phenomenon has been facilitated by the birthing of the cell based church model. There have been explosions of growth in places like Singapore, the Ivory Coast and Bogota Colombia, where churches of up to 90,000 are being reported. Various models have been employed in different places, but one thing is certain and that is that Jesus is visiting His church afresh through the vehicle of cells.

One of the characteristics of these cells is – 'ice breakers'. To this end Michael Puffett and Sheldon Rottler have compiled this excellent book.

Both the authors have extensive experience with cells both in larger and smaller churches, Michael having operated two very successful zones in the large Harvest Church in Port Elizabeth, before taking up the senior pastorship of the Queenstown Christian Centre where cells are now operating successfully. Sheldon has administered cells in both of these situations.

Having known and worked with both authors personally for several years and enjoyed the privilege of observing their enthusiasm for cell life within the local church, I believe that their expertise will be of great blessing to your cell or church.

David and Carol Cape

1
FUN ICE-BREAKERS

Ten tips for fun ice-breakers

1. Preparation is the key to successful fun ice-breakers.
2. Use the element of surprise, ie don't be predictable; keep the cell members guessing about what is going to happen in the cell meeting — it adds excitement to any cell meeting.
3. Avoid making comments such as: 'We are now going to do a fun ice-breaker.' Allow the evening to flow naturally.
4. Use 'volunteers' who are likely not to get embarrassed doing the ice-breaker.
5. Make sure you understand the rules of the ice-breaker properly — this will avoid embarrassing situations.
6. Explain any rules carefully and properly. Repeat the instructions until everyone understands.
7. Make sure that the ice-breaker *always* remains fun, ie don't let a competitive spirit develop.
8. Make sure you have all your equipment for the ice-breaker ready so that no time is wasted during the cell meeting looking for the materials required.
9. Attempt to include everyone in the ice-breaker in one way or another — especially visitors or anyone feeling left out or uncomfortable.
10. Be enthusiastic as you lead the fun ice-breaker.

1 Memory mania

Each player needs a piece of paper and a pencil for this activity. The cell leader places on a tray a large variety of items of all shapes, sizes and uses. In fact, the more the merrier. The tray is then covered with a cloth and carried into the room where the players are waiting. The cloth is taken off and the players have thirty seconds in which to make a mental note of all the objects on the tray. However, no one is

11

allowed to write anything down at this stage. The tray is then removed and the players are given one minute to write down all the items they can remember seeing. The winner is the person who can remember the most objects.

2 Pick up toothpicks

Have enough toothpicks for your group. Drop all the toothpicks in a bunch and take turns to go around and draw out a stick without disturbing the bundle. If you move another stick, you skip a turn. The winner is the person who has collected the most sticks at the end. If you draw out one stick successfully, you may continue until a stick moves. Motivate all your members to play.

3 Balloon annihilation

Give each person in the cell two balloons and two pieces of string, approximately forty centimetres long. They must blow up the balloons and tie one around each ankle. The object of the game is to pop the other cell members' balloons while protecting your own from being popped. The winner is the last person to have an un-popped balloon.

4 Missing words

Divide the cell into groups of three or four and give each group a copy of this puzzle.

One day on the Isle of _____ — it was _____ that _____ if I recall — I was standing looking out over the _____ when I saw a terrible _____. Billy and Bertha were having a _____.

Bertha had said, 'Billy, you're _____!' And Billy replied with a slur, 'Bertha, you know, you just _____ be _____!'

Find the nine missing words in this short paragraph. Apart from the first letter of each word, they are all spelt the same way, eg waste, paste, taste, etc.

Answers in Solutions section.

5 Treasure hunt

Divide the cell into two or three groups, depending on the size of your cell, and play a game of treasure hunt. Before the meeting, meet with your intern and think up some really thought-provoking riddles that lead on from each other. For example, the first riddle is given to each team. They must then solve the first riddle that will lead them to the second riddle hidden somewhere in the house, the garden or in town. The last riddle leads them to the prize. (The teams must have riddles that lead them to different places, ie no two teams must go to the same place. However, the last riddle of each team must be the same, leading them to the single prize.) Therefore the first team to solve all the riddles will get the prize. Have a prize that is not too expensive but enough for the group to share.

6 Musical clothes

Place a number of 'different' clothing items in a black bag. Items such as: boxer running shorts, rugby boots, a pair of socks with holes in them, underpants, petticoat, stockings, gloves, etc. (Be creative.) About sixteen to twenty items in total. Someone either plays a tape recorder or guitar while the bag is passed slowly around the circle. Every time the music stops, the person who has the bag must remove an item of clothing and put it on over their clothes. Do this until the bag is empty. This should break up quite a bit of ice and get a couple of laughs.

7 African adventure

This is a competition between the cells to see who knows the most African countries. Divide into small groups and give

each a photocopy of the map above. Get each group to write as many countries as they can. Ask people not to cheat. When you have finished, collect the sheets to see how many countries you have correctly identified and fill it in on your cell leader's report.

Answers in Solutions section (pp. 134).

8 *Find the leader*

Have your group sit in a circle. A person chosen as 'It' closes his eyes, while someone in the circle is chosen to be the leader. Then, while 'It' tries to identify the leader, the participants in the circle copy motions such as clapping hands, clicking fingers, stamping feet, etc., always watching the leader to see what action to copy and only doing actions that the leader initiates.

The leader is caught when 'It' catches him/her giving an action to copy. As soon as the leader is caught he/she goes into the centre and becomes 'It'.

9 Check your mate

Organise a game of check your mate with your cell. How you do it is up to you.

Husband	Wife
What is your wife's favourite colour?	What is your favourite colour?
What is your favourite meal?	What is your husband's favourite meal?
What type of flowers does your wife like the most?	What type of flowers do you like the most?
What chocolate do you like best?	What chocolate does your husband like best?
If money were no object, what would your wife desire to have most?	If money were no object, what would you desire to have most?
If you had the time and the money, which two countries would you most like to visit?	If you had the time and the money, which two countries would your husband most like to visit.
In bad weather, what would your wife really hate to be out in — rain or wind?	In bad weather, what would you really hate to be out in — rain or wind?
What do you normally like to do for relaxation after a hard day at work?	What does your husband like to do to relax after a hard day at work?
What characteristic do you most appreciate about your wife?	What characteristic do you think your husband most appreciates about you?
Do you polish your own shoes?	Does your husband polish his own shoes?
Where did you first meet your wife?	Where did your husband first meet you?
Do you usually remember anniversaries and birthdays?	Does your husband usually remember anniversaries and birthdays?

10 Killer

Have the group sit in a circle. Get them
to close their eyes and you appoint a
killer. When they open their eyes pick
someone to be 'It'. 'It' stands
in the centre of the circle
and has to identify the killer.
    The killer kills by winking
at a person. When someone
is killed, they must enact the most
dramatic death possible to generate laughter. Once the killer
is identified, 'It' sits down and the killer takes his or her place
in the centre of the circle as 'It'. Appoint a new killer.
    Tell the group that if they have ever wanted to get involved
in a career of acting, this is their opportunity.

11 Shadrach, Meshach and Abed-nego

This game will take a little concentration, so explain it well
the first time. Each contestant is called Shadrach. The person
sitting on his right is Meshach. The person on his left is Abed-
nego. Someone who is 'It' stands in the centre.
    'It' points to someone seated. Suppose he points at you,
the person sitting on your right is Michael Puffett (Meshach).
The person sitting on your left is Sheldon Rottler (Abed-nego).
'It' calls, 'Meshach!' Before 'It' can count to ten, you must
shout out the name 'Michael Puffett'.

12 Newspaper squash

Divide your group into two teams (men against women might
work well). Depending on the size of the teams, give them
one or two pages of newspaper. Place the paper on the floor.
Each team must huddle together and stand on the piece of
paper within a certain time period. Once successful, the size
of the paper is halved and the exercise repeated. The team
that has the most people standing on the smallest piece of
paper is the winner.

13 Baby face

Ask each cell member to bring along a photograph of themselves as a baby. Display all the photographs and have a competition to see who can identify the people in the photographs. The person with the most correct answers wins.

14 Apple bobbing and Smartie (M and M) search

Beforehand, prepare two or three bowls of water with an apple in them and a bowl of flour with about twenty Smarties in it.

Choose contestants, one per bowl of water and flour, and let them compete against each other and against time to see how many Smarties they can retrieve from the flour — they must not eat the Smarties.

However, before they can search for a Smartie, they have to take a bite of the apple without using their hands. Have a box of Smarties as a prize for the winner.

This is a messy game, so choose appropriate contestants as it can become embarrassing for some people.

15 Humility contest

Give each of your guests six ribbons of various colours to pin on their chests or lapels. No guest is to say, 'I' for the rest of the evening. If one guest catches another guest saying, 'I', he/she is entitled to take one of that guest's ribbons. The one having the most ribbons at the end of the game receives a prize for his/her contribution towards the cause of humility.

NB: It might be a good idea to start this game before you have your coffee/tea time. Stop the game before you go into praise and worship or edification time.

16 Dots

For this game you will need a grid of evenly spaced dots, similar to that shown below.

Each player takes a turn to draw either a horizontal or vertical line thereby joining two dots. Whenever a player draws a line that completes a block, they claim that block by writing their initials inside it. Completing a block allows that person another turn. The winner is the person who at the end of the game has claimed the most blocks.

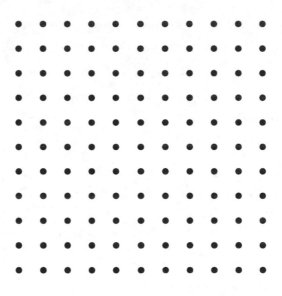

17 I packed my trunk for China

The first player says, 'I packed my trunk for China and took an apple (or any other object that begins with an 'A'). The next player repeats the sentence, including the 'A' word and adds a 'B' word. Each successive player recites the sentence with all the alphabetical items, adding one of his/her own which would be from the next letter of the alphabet. Try to continue play until the alphabet is completed.

18 Spanish inquisition

Choose a few couples to play this game in front of everybody. The game begins with the first person asking the second person a question. The second person has to answer the first person with a 'logical' question following on from the first … and so on. The loser is the first person to give a straight answer.

A typical game might go as follows:

Peter: Where are you going?
Jill: What's it got to do with you?
Peter: Am I not allowed to ask?
Jill: I don't know … aren't you?
Peter: Don't you know me well enough to answer? Etc.

It might be a good idea to play men against women.

19 Stop press

This ice-breaker requires a bit of planning beforehand. Get a pile of old newspapers and rearrange the pages of each one so that they do not run in sequence; one newspaper for each player.

Have chairs set out, one per cell member, in two straight lines facing each other with just sufficient room for two people to sit facing one another and one chair at each end.

Once the cell members have taken their seats, give them their newspapers and instruct them to get the pages in order. The winner is the first person to get his/her paper neatly in the correct order.

20 Cell IQ test

Hand out copies of the following 'IQ test'. Each block represents a well-known phrase or saying. Divide your group into teams of two or three. Give a time limit. The team with the most correct answers wins. Have some sort of prize for the winning group.

PLASMA H$_2$O	1	HIGH CLOUDS	2	1 3 5 7 9 WHELMING	3
EILNPU	4	PICT RES	5	WRITING	6
ARREST YOU'RE	7	LESODUB TENNIS	8	KJUSTK	9
B ILL ED	10	GETTINGITALL	11	1 T 3 4 5 6	12
24 HOURS	13	T RN	14	LOV	15

1. _____   2. _____

3. _____   4. _____

5. _____   6. _____

7. _____   8. _____

9. _____   10. _____

11. _____   12. _____

13. _____   14. _____

15. _____

Answers in Solutions section.

21 Charades

Choose a variety of titles from movies, stage plays, songs, television shows, etc.

When playing charades, divide the cell into two teams (men and women). Have them competing against each other for some sort of prize — even if it is just their dignity and pride.

The teams sit completely separate. Each team now sends a representative to the cell leader, who just shows them a card with the title on it. They read the card and return to the team without saying a word. They now act out the statement and the group must keep guessing until they get the statement in full, correct. The judge's decision is final.

22 Hangman

Play a few rounds of hangman. As the cell leader, choose words that are not too easy, yet not too difficult. Get a volunteer from the group to challenge you. If they are not able to get the word, they have to pay some sort of forfeit. If they do get the word, you have to do the forfeit. Be a sport and let them get a couple of words correct.

23 Needle threading race

Men against women. Get two volunteers from each sex. Don't tell them what they will be doing. Each person must thread four needles, against time. The winner is the person who threads all four needles in the shortest time. Have a small prize for the winner.

24 Bizz-buzz

This game will test your mathematical skills. All the players must arrange themselves in a circle. The first player calls out the number 'one', the second player the number 'two', the third player...well, this is where the game gets complicated.

In bizz-buzz, the number three is outlawed. Any word containing the number three or a multiple thereof must be replaced with the word bizz.

An even more exciting version of the game is to outlaw the number seven as well. Any word containing the number seven or a multiple thereof must be replaced with the word buzz.

If a number contains both three and seven (thirty-seven) or a multiple of three and seven (twenty-one), the player must say bizz-buzz.

A player who makes a mistake must drop out. Play can continue until either the agreed upon target is reached or there is only one player left in the game.

25 Bible quiz

Play a twenty-question Bible quiz with the men competing against the women. Write up the score — have a prize for the winning team and have the losing team serve coffee and cake at the following cell meeting.

26 Noughts and crosses

Play a knockout round of noughts and crosses. For a variation, play doubles, ie two people in a team, alternating their moves, against another two people doing the same.

27 Knot quite right

Everybody stand in a circle. Reach across the circle and grab somebody's right hand with your left hand and somebody else's left hand with your right hand. Do not let go at all. Try and untangle the 'knot' so that the circle is unravelled. *It is possible!*

28 Wild evaluations

Everyone chooses a partner whom they do not know very well. Each person should have a piece of paper and a pencil at hand. Without talking to their partner, they are to guess the following items concerning him/her:

- his/her favourite food
- his/her favourite colour
- his/her perfume/deodorant
- his/her ultimate career (use your imagination)
- his/her wildest dream
- the last time they got angry. When was it, or what was it about?

Give five minutes to write these answers down without talking. When they are finished, compare the answers. See who gets the most correct answers.

29 Banana duel

Let the cell divide up into pairs and tie their left wrists together. Give each person a banana to hold in their left hand. At the word 'Go' they peel the banana with only their right hands and try to push it in their partner's face/mouth.

As a variation, you may want to do this blindfolded to add to the excitement.

30 Broken telephone

The cell leader whispers something in the first person's ear. That person then relates the message to the following person in the circle. The last person then speaks the message out aloud. (Once the person has passed on the message, it cannot be repeated.) The cell leader then repeats the message that he originally started. (The statement to be repeated is designed to be lengthy.)

Pass this message along the chain:

'Meet me at four o'clock on the corner of Seventh Avenue and Fifth Avenue. Bring along eight friends and five pounds because we are going to walk to the eight till late shop in Tenth Avenue to buy fourteen apples and six bananas. Whatever you do, don't tell a soul!'

31 Pair up

Write different names on sticky labels. The names must be ones everyone knows, and ones which can be coupled, eg:

Mickey Mouse and Minnie Mouse
Bonnie and Clyde
Adam and Eve
Tarzan and Jane.

As the people arrive, paste a name on their backs (do not let them see the name and tell them not to ask anyone what the name is). When you do the ice-breaker, everyone must move around the room asking questions to find out who they are. The questions they may ask can only have a Yes/No answer. Once they know who they are, they must find their partner.

Use them in their pairs to discuss questions pertaining to the rest of the cell meeting.

32 Knockout staring competition

Divide into pairs and stare at each other until one person blinks. Winners then divide into pairs. Do this until there are only two left in the final round. Let the rest of the cell cheer on the two 'starers'. Have a small prize for the winner.

33 Dictionary

Play two rounds of balderdash. Here are two words for you to use:

ZEBECK   meaning: light Mediterranean vessel.
TINTINNABULATION   meaning: ringing of bells.

Explain very carefully how the game is played. Each person has a piece of paper. On the top of their piece of paper they must write their own name. The cell leader also does this. The cell leader then calls out the first word and spells it out. Everyone must write down the word and propose a meaning, definition or explanation of the word. (NB: your definition must be so convincing that it seems like the correct answer.) Meanwhile the cell leader has also written down the word and the correct definition. He/she collects all the pieces of paper, making sure that he/she can read all the handwriting. He/she shuffles all the definitions, including the correct one, then reads them out as if all are correct. Each person then chooses which one they think is the right definition. The person whose definition is chosen the most wins. After they have all chosen which definition they think is correct, reveal the correct definition.

Scoring is as follows:

3 points if they choose the correct definition;

2 points for each person who chooses your definition;

5 points to the leader if no one chooses the correct definition.

34   Pegs on a line

Before the meeting starts, set up this ice-breaker.

Run a piece of strong string the full length of the room, tying it at both ends at shoulder height. Place forty clothes pegs on the line, with two buckets under the line two metres apart from each other. Divide the cell into two teams (eg men against women).

The aim of the game is for a team to get as many pegs into their bucket before all the pegs have been used. At the word go, both teams must, using their mouths, take the pegs off the string and drop them into the buckets. If a peg drops on the floor, they must pick it up with their mouths. When all the pegs arc taken off the line, count the pegs in each bucket. The winner is the team with the most pegs.

35   The essence of smell

Divide into two teams. Get hold of approximately ten fruits that have a scent, or different food essences used for cooking.

Blindfold a member of each team and ask them to come forward to smell. (You can have different people come forward for each fruit.) The team with the most correct answers wins. Have a forfeit prize for the losing team, eg serving the other team coffee and cake at the next cell meeting.

Have the cell comment on what their favourite fruit is and why.

36   Four-in-a-row chair game

Divide the cell into two equal teams (men against women is normally easiest for this game). The aim of the game is to get four members from one team sitting next to each other.

To start, let's use an example of a cell group of twelve people, six men and six women. Sit in a circle of man, woman, man, woman all the way round. Decide which four seats are going to be used as the winning seats. Write numbers from one to twelve on small pieces of paper, fold them and put them in a hat. Each person picks a number and no one must see your number. There must always be an empty chair in the circle (ie there should originally be thirteen chairs).

Now the game can start. The person who has the empty chair on their left calls out any number between one and twelve. The person with the corresponding number gets up and sits on the empty chair and swaps their number with the caller. Both remain in their chairs. The person who now has the empty chair on their left calls out the next number and so the game continues. The object is to memorise who has what number so as to get four from the same team sitting next to each other, on the winning seats.

37   Jam and cottonwool relay

Put your cell into two relay teams. Place a blob of jam on each person's nose. On the word 'go', a piece of cottonwool is passed from one person's nose to the next (without using their hands). The first team to complete this funny relay wins.

38   Up we go

Divide the cell into twos (men with men, women with women). Sit on the floor with feet on the floor, back to back, link arms and try to stand up. Time the teams and give the winning team a small prize.

39   Weather report

Go around the cell and let each person describe their week so far by means of a weather report, using weather terminology, eg fine, mild, cloudy, stormy, gales, high or low pressures, etc. Let the cell then explain why their week was like that.

40   Straw chew

Give each cell member a straw. Have them put the straw in their mouths. The object of the game is to get the entire straw into their mouths only using their lips and tongue.

41   Elastic band

Give each cell member an elastic band. Have them put it around their head going over their nose. The object is to use facial muscles to get the elastic band around their neck.

42   Baby photo quiz

Have each cell member bring a photograph of themselves as a baby to the cell meeting. Make a collage of the photos and have the cell guess who the person in the photograph is and why they say so.

43   Camping trip

You are going on a three-day camping trip up in the mountains. You will carry everything you need for the three days in a pack on your back. Since you are going into the mountains, it will be cold. You have decided that you cannot carry more than 5 kgs on your back comfortably. You have made a list of things that you want to take with you but they amount to more than 15 kgs.

Now you have to read the list and include only the most important items, totalling a weight of 15 kgs, to survive the three days without seeing anyone.

Come to a decision in your group and explain why you chose the items on your list (be sure that they amount to no more than 15 kgs). When you have finished compiling your list, share with the rest of the cell what you will be taking. You may challenge or be challenged by another group to explain why you chose an item, so be sure that you can justify each item.

3 kg sleeping bag	50 g matches
1½ kg back pack	1 kg pillow
250 g dish soap	250 g toothpaste
½ kg cooking pot	½ kg torch
3 kg water container (filled)	125 g toothbrush
2 kg extra pair of shoes	2 kg camera
3 kg 3-day food supply	1 kg eating utensils
1 kg insect repellent	2 kg fishing rod
2 kg extra set of clothing	½ kg swim suit
½ kg rain jacket	½ kg towel
½ kg small book to record what you see	

44   *Actionary*

Actionary is played on the same principle as 'Pictionary', however, instead of drawing a picture, the word is acted out. When playing 'Actionary', divide the cell into two teams (men and women). Have them play against each other for some sort of prize — even if it is just their dignity and pride.

The teams sit completely separately. Each team now sends a representative to the cell leader, who just shows them a card on which a word is written. They read the word and return to the team without saying anything. They now act out the word and the group must keep guessing until they get the word correct. The judge's decision is final.

45 Drinking relay

Divide the cell into groups of four or five people. Give each group a jug containing a litre of cold drink and each cell member a straw. The object of the game is to be the first group to finish the cold drink by drinking it through the straw.

46 Fun debate

Divide the cell into two teams. Choose a controversial topic, eg abortion, the death penalty, reincarnation, etc. Have the two teams debate the subject — one team pro the topic and the other team anti the topic.

47 Hand full of beans

Give each cell member five beans. Instruct them to go around the room collecting beans from the other cell members by asking them questions. If anybody answers a question with 'Yes' or 'No', they have to forfeit a bean to the person asking the question. The winner is the person with the most beans at the end of the game.

For variation, this game can be played with shoes. Have the cell members remove their shoes and play the game in the same manner as with the beans.

48 Paper emotions

Give each cell member a piece of paper and have them express the way that they are feeling with the piece of paper. Eg they might crumple the paper to show frustration or anxiety, tear up the paper to show anger, stand on the paper to show pressure or stress, etc.

Divide into pairs and pray for each other for a release of any negative emotions.

49 Bible draw

Prepare a few scriptures before the cell meeting (at least ten to fifteen scriptures). Play the game by reading a scripture out aloud. The object is to see which cell member can find the scripture first. Award five points per correct answer. The winner will be the person with the highest score. Have a small prize for the winner.

50 Scripture buns

This ice-breaker is going to require a bit of baking.

On small pieces of paper, write the scriptures that you will be using for your edification time (one scripture per piece of paper). Make two of each scripture. Laminate the pieces of paper with the scripture on, either with Sellotape or contact and place it inside the raw mixture of a bun. Bake the buns.

During the coffee/tea time, hand out the buns, one per person, informing the cell members to find something inside their bun which they must hold on to. Then instruct them to find the person with the corresponding scripture and spend the rest of the cell meeting with that person.

During your edification time, have the cell members read out the scriptures which they found in their buns.

51   Guess the song

This ice-breaker requires a bit of preparation before the meeting.

On a blank audio cassette, record five to ten-second introductions of a number of well-known songs (modern and old). Divide the cell into teams and have them play against each other for a small prize.

Play the song and the first group to respond correctly is awarded five points. If a team responds incorrectly, subtract two points from their total.

The winning team is the one with the most points at the end of the game.

52   Candle relay

Divide the cell into two teams. Divide each of the teams into two and have them stand on opposite sides of the room or opposite each other outside in the garden — ready for a relay race.

Give each person a candle. Give the first person in each team, a box of matches and get them to kneel and light their candle. The object is, at the word 'Go', for the second person in that team to light their candle from the person kneeling and run to their team on the opposite side and light the first person's candle. That person then has to run back to the first group and light the next person's candle. This carries on until everyone's candle is lit. The winning team is the one whose candles are all lit first.

If a candle blows out while they are running to their team on the opposite side, they have to go back to the person who originally lit their candle.

Use this ice-breaker on the theme of either 'Jesus being the light of the world' or to illustrate the statement: 'Each one, reach one and touch the world!'

53 The fax machine

Give each cell member a piece of paper and a pencil. Divide the cell into pairs and have them sit back to back. One of the players draws a very simple picture, eg a house, a car, etc. on his sheet of paper. He then describes his drawing to his partner, without using shapes, symbols, etc., who in turn has to attempt to duplicate the drawing without seeing it. Once they have completed the drawing, they have to identify the object.

54 General knowledge quiz

Have a general knowledge quiz. Make this a game between men and women. The prize for the winners is that the losing group has to serve coffee/tea to the winning team.

Questions

1. Name the highest waterfall in the world.
2. Which planet is fifth furthest from the sun.
3. What colour is citrine?
4. When a ship shows the 'blue peter', what is it about to do?
5. How many moons does Uranus have?
6. Who first designed the helicopter?
7. Which breed of dog is usually associated with the Queen?
8. Which two countries compete for 'the Ashes'?
9. Name the missing colour: red, orange, yellow, green, blue, violet.
10. What is the currency of Russia?
11. Where is your patella?
12. What instrument measures atmospheric pressure?
13. How many carats are there in pure gold?
14. Who won the 1995 rugby world cup?
15. Name the capital of Australia.
16. What is the third last book of the Old Testament?

17. In which country was cricketer, Tony Grieg, born?
18. Where were the 1988 Winter Olympics held?
19. What do the carats in diamonds measure?
20. What is a palindrome?

Answers in Solutions chapter.

55 *True or false*

Questions

1. The old Orient Express ran between Istanbul and London.
2. Astigmatism affects the eyes.
3. The modern name for brimstone is ash.
4. NASA stands for North American Space Agency.
5. Helium, as an element, has the highest boiling point.
6. A female elephant is called a cow.
7. Ferrets cannot catch a cold.
8. Former Israeli Prime Minister, David Ben Gurion, was born David Green.
9. Absalom succeeded his father, David, as king.
10. If you were a Selenite, you would be living in Slovenia.
11. Britain abolished slavery in 1834.
12. Apple pips contain the deadly poison, cyanide.
13. Kangaroo meat is rich in cholesterol.
14. The first human heart transplant occurred in 1967.
15. China has the world's most crowded railway system.
16. A Bactrian camel has two humps.
17. King Henry VIII had five wives.
18. Moses was ordered to take the animals into the ark two by two.
19. Karl Marx died in 1883.
20. The book of Revelations was written by John the Baptist.

Answers in Solutions chapter.

56 Shoe in the box

Divide the cell into two or more teams. Place a large box approximately ten metres away from the contestants. Give each person from the team an opportunity to kick each of their shoes off into the box. When one team is finished, count the number of shoes in the box. Give the rest of the teams a chance and announce the winner as the team with the most shoes in the box.

57 Capital questions

Divide the cell into two teams and see who is able to name the most capitals. The first letter of each capital is provided.

1.	Algeria	A	_____
2.	Belgium	B	_____
3.	Canada	O	_____
4.	Denmark	C	_____
5.	Somalia	M	_____
6.	Poland	W	_____
7.	Wales	C	_____
8.	Lebanon	B	_____
9.	Malawi	L	_____
10.	Nigeria	L	_____
11.	Spain	M	_____
12.	Australia	C	_____
13.	Uganda	K	_____
14.	Venezuela	C	_____
15.	Turkey	A	_____
16.	Yemen (South)	A	_____
17.	Bulgaria	S	_____
18.	Romania	B	_____
19.	Jordan	A	_____
20.	Hungary	B	_____

Answers in Solutions chapter.

58   Cotton throw

This is an ideal indoor ice-breaker. Make a ball out of soft
fluffy cottonwool. Mark out a line on the floor and get each
cell member to throw the cotton ball as far as they can. Have
a small prize for the person who can throw the ball the
farthest.

59   Twenty questions

Have one person from the group choose a 'teaser': an object,
place, person or thing. The rest of the group ask questions to
identify what the object, etc., is. However, the questions may
only be answered with a 'Yes' or 'No'. An outright guess, eg
'Are you Queen Elizabeth?' is counted as a question. The
player who correctly identifies the teaser has the opportunity
to set the next teaser. If no one guesses correctly, the
original player gets to set a second teaser.

60   Who am I?

Played on the same principle as 'Twenty Questions', the
person setting the teaser chooses a prominent figure, dead or
alive, real or fictional, eg Elton John, James Bond, Bill Clinton,
Princess Diana, etc., only announcing the initial of that
person's name. The rest of the group then has to identify who
the person is.

   If the person's identity has not been established after
twenty questions, the original player has an opportunity to
choose another character. He carries on until someone has
correctly identified the character. The player who correctly
identified the character decides on the next character and
answers the group's questions.

61 Bull's-eye

Place a chair in the middle of the room with an empty bottle behind the chair. Each cell member gets a chance to kneel on the chair and attempt to drop six clothes pegs through the opening of the bottle. One strict rule is that no one may drop their hand further than the top of the chair's back rest.

62 Hangman

Before the cell meeting, write a number of lengthy words on a piece of paper (one word per piece of paper), eg ESTABLISHMENT, CONGREGATION, ENCYCLOPAEDIA, etc.

Draw a dash for each letter in the word as shown below:

E S T A B L I S H M E N T

The rest of the group call out letters of the alphabet. If they choose a letter that appears in the word, that letter is filled in on the correct dash. For example, if someone calls out the letter 'E', fill in the following:

E _ _ _ _ _ _ _ _ _ E _ _

If they call out incorrect letters, start to draw the hangman picture in ten stages:

1. The base
2. The vertical bar
3. The horizontal bar
4. The rope
5. The head
6. The body
7. The first arm
8. The second arm
9. The first leg
10. The second leg.

The game continues either until the group guesses the word or the diagram is completed.

63 Eye contact

For this ice-breaker you will need to find photographs of famous people from magazines.

Cut out the eyes from the photographs and paste them onto a piece of cardboard. (For your own record, make a note of which eyes belong to whom.) Give the cell a list of names of the characters whose eyes you have pasted on the cardboard, including some names of other people who are not featured. The winner of the game is the person who correctly identifies all the eyes of the characters.

64 Consequences 1

Divide the cell into groups of seven. Give each group a single piece of paper and tell them to fold it into seven equal parts. The first person draws some sort of headgear on the first folded section without any of the other team members seeing. That section is then folded back only exposing two lines where the next person has to continue drawing. The paper is passed on to the second person who draws the head and neck. Then the third person draws the chest and waist. The fourth person draws the centre section. The fifth person draws the thighs and knees. The sixth person draws the shins and ankles and lastly the seventh person draws the feet. Each time the paper is folded back to hide the previous person's drawing, and only exposing the two lines where the next person has to start their drawing.

When all the players have completed their sections, the paper is unfolded to expose their work of art.

65 Consequences 2

Played on the same principle as Consequences 1, with the variation being, instead of drawing, the players write a short story in nine stages.

Divide the cell into groups of nine. Give each group a

single piece of paper and tell them to fold it into nine equal parts. After each person has written their part, they fold that section backwards, hidden from the next player.

The stages are as follows:

1. A description of a man
2. The name of this man
3. A description of a woman
4. The name of this woman
5. The place where they met
6. What the man gave the woman
7. What the man said to the woman
8. What the woman said to the man
9. What happened as a result of their meeting.

When all these stages have been completed, the page is unfolded and the stories are read aloud to the group.

66 Paper-cutting race

Divide the cell into small groups and give each group a sheet of newspaper and some glue. Have them put glue on the top left-hand corner of the newspaper and then stick the sheet onto the wall. Give each group a pair of scissors and instruct them to cut the sheet into one long strip that will reach to the other side of the room. The first team to do so is the winner. However, any team that breaks their strand is automatically disqualified.

67 Irish crossword puzzle

1	2	3	4	5
6				
7				
8				
9				

Clues

Across	Down
1. Vegetables	1. Judy's friend
6. Female sheep	2. A boxing blow
7. They lay eggs	3. A party refreshment
8. Oceans	4. It makes holes
9. Cockneys drop them	5. A British magazine

68 Tie relay

Divide all the men of the cell into two equal teams. Give each team one tie and instruct them that the object is for each person to put on the tie properly, undo it and pass it onto the next player who does the same until all the players have completed the exercise. The  winning team is the first team to have all their members put on and undo the tie. Assign two of the women to be judges making sure that the tie is properly put on and undone before passed onto the next player.

69 Power of observation

Have your cell make a thorough observation of your lounge or room where you have your cell meeting. Lead them out of the room into another room in the house. While they are out, make some alterations to the lounge, eg move a lamp from one part of the room to another, move a rug, draw or open the curtains, remove or add magazines, etc. Be sure to make a note of the changes yourself.

Have the cell members come back into the lounge and write down all the changes that they can see. The winner is the person who can identify the most changes.

70 Vocabulary experts

Have the cell sit in a circle and appoint one person to be 'It' who stands in the centre of the circle. 'It' points to someone in the circle and calls out a letter, possibly with the exception of 'X'. That person then has to call out a proper name (person's name, country, river, etc.) starting with that letter. You may want to restrict it to Bible characters. If the person cannot answer in the time that 'It' counts to a certain number, which is decided before the game starts, the person then becomes 'It' and the game continues.

71 Bible spelling test

Have an old-fashioned spelling test, using names and places from the Bible.

A good idea is to have the men competing against the women.

72 Fruit basket

Have the cell sit in a circle. Divide them into four equal groups by giving them each a number from one to four. Inform the ones that they are oranges, the twos that they are lemons, the threes that they are bananas and the fours that they are apples.

Have a person who is 'It' stand in the centre of the circle and call out one of these four fruits. All the people belonging to that fruit group have to get up and quickly change places with another person of the same group while the other fruits remain seated. While the change is in progress, 'It' tries to steal one of the open chairs. If he/she succeeds, the person left standing becomes 'It' and the person who was 'It' becomes part of that fruit group.

Occasionally 'It' will call out, 'fruit basket.' When the person does this, everybody has to get up and swap places with each other. The person left standing when everyone is seated becomes 'It'.

73 Bible vocabulary

Have your cell sit in a circle and appoint someone to be 'It'. During the game, 'It' points to a person in the circle and calls out either 'city', 'country', 'man' or 'maid'. The person in the circle has to reply with a name from the Bible of one of the above.

The game can go something like this: If 'It' points to someone and shouts, 'City,' the person in the circle can reply with 'Jerusalem.' If 'It' shouted, 'Man,' the person could reply, 'Joshua.' If the person cannot answer in the time that 'It' counts to a certain number, which is decided before the game starts, the person then becomes 'It' and the game continues.

74 Sense of touch

Each cell member is given a sack or a packet containing an equal number of objects such as an apple, a spoon, a stick of chewing gum, a tennis ball, etc.

The cell leader calls out an object and the cell members have to reach into the bag and remove that object without looking in the bag, before the leader counts to ten. If they succeed in bringing out the correct object, they place it to one side. If they do not succeed the object remains in the bag. The aim of the game is to see who can remove the most objects that are called out.

75   Kill-joy

Line up all the male cell members along the wall. Then get all the women to try and make the men smile. If they smile they are removed from the line and join the women in trying to make the rest of the men smile.

Give this a surprise ending by awarding a booby prize to the man that remains standing the longest, saying that he has been named the biggest kill-joy at the cell.

You might want to ask for volunteers for this game so as not to embarrass any newcomers to the cell.

76   Know your merchandise

Write down a number of slogans from companies that advertise well-known products. Read these slogans to your cell members and see if they can guess what the product is or who the manufacturer is.

77   Shoe box

Have a box at the front door as your cell members arrive. Each person has one attempt at kicking both their shoes into the box from a distance of five to ten metres. If they succeed in getting their shoes in, they may wear them as normal. Whichever shoe does not go into the box is forfeited and that person has to walk around without that shoe on for a time period that you decide on before their shoes are returned. If they miss the box with both shoes, they have to remain without shoes for that duration of time.

78   Copy cat

Take two soup plates and blacken the bottom of one over a candle flame. Put a little water in each so as to fool your prey as to what is going to happen.

As your cell members arrive, have them sit down with you and instruct them to look you squarely in the eyes and do exactly what you do. Have someone hand you the clean soup bowl and hand your cell member the blackened one. Have your cell member do all sorts of things and then gradually have him take his/her dirty fingers, which he/she will be unaware of, from underneath the dish and make all sorts of smudge marks on his/her face.

79   A-tissue

Divide the cell into two teams and give each team a tissue and each team member a straw. Have the team stand in a straight line. The leaders of the teams start sucking on their straws and place the tissue at the end of the straw. The object of the game is to pass the tissue from person to person by sucking it from straw to straw.

80   Bucket of potatoes

Place a large bucket against the wall and ask for volunteers from the cell who think that they have got a good eye. Give them a dozen potatoes and instruct them to try and throw the potatoes into the bucket while blindfolded.

When they are blindfolded and ready to throw the first potato, get another cell member to silently pick up the bucket and catch their first potato in it. The bucket is now removed until the twelfth potato is once again caught inside the bucket. All the while, the rest of the cell members are shouting words of encouragement to the frustrated contestant who cannot understand why they are missing the mark so many times.

When they take off their blindfolds, they will wonder why they came so close and only managed to get two potatoes in the bucket. Do not reveal your secret until the end of the evening.

81 Chronological order

Have a number of chronological questions in the form of
people or events ready before the cell meeting. Have your cell
sit in a circle and go around the circle giving each person a
chance to answer a question.

The questions are based on time periods as to what or
who came first. For example, you might give two names,
'Peter or Paul?' The contestant then has to answer who came
first. The answer would naturally be Peter, as he made his
appearance in the Gospels and Paul only emerged in the book
of Acts. If the two subjects were, for example, 'Tower of Babel
or Walls of Jericho?', the answer would be 'Tower of Babel'.

82 Name the book quiz

Select a number of Bible incidents from the Old and New
Testament. Divide your cell into two teams and quiz them
against each other awarding five points for a correct answer
and two points for a question that has been passed on from
the other team. Have your cell guess from which book in the
Bible the incident is extracted, telling them that no book will
be used twice.

Have a small prize for the winning team.

83 Bible verse errors

Read a Bible story to your cell, making deliberate errors such
as incorrect names of people, incorrect places, etc. Have your
cell members identify the errors and write them down. The
winner is the person who correctly identifies the most errors.

Award five points for correctly recognising a mistake and
subtract two points if they identify a mistake that was actually
correct.

Make sure that you have all the errors written down
beforehand so that you do not get confused.

84   Mummy

Divide the cell into two equal
teams. Have each team
appoint a leader. Give each
team a roll of toilet paper
and instruct them to wrap
their leader in the toilet
paper. The winning team
is the first to completely
wrap their leader.

85   Fetch my shoe

Divide the cell into pairs. Have the cell sitting in a circle with
one person from the pair sitting on a chair and the other
sitting blindfolded on the floor in front of them facing towards
the inside of the circle. The person sitting on the chair
removes one of his/her shoes, which is placed in the centre
of the circle. At the word go, the people sitting on the floor
then have to fetch their partner's shoe, directed only by their
partner's voice giving directions. The winner is the first
person to correctly retrieve their partner's shoe.

86   The winking game

Have the cell pair off one man and one woman together. Let
all the women in the cell sit on chairs in a circle with the men
standing behind them. There must be one chair vacant with a
man standing behind it. He is 'It'.

The object is for 'It' to get one of the women to come and
sit on his chair by winking at her. She has to try and escape
from where she is sitting before the man behind her grabs her
shoulders. If she manages to escape, the man with the open
chair becomes 'It'.

87 Framed

Choose a volunteer to stand in front of the cell holding an empty frame in front of his mournfully expressive face. The purpose of the exercise is for the rest of the cell to attempt to change that person's expression within one minute. Each cell member has a chance at being 'framed' and the winner is anyone lasting the minute without twitching.

88 Can you do this?

Have the cell sit in a circle. One person starts this activity by performing a particular action such as pulling a face, jumping up and down, standing on one leg, etc. The next person in the circle has to imitate the action of the first person with the addition of his/her own action. The third person then has to repeat the first two actions and add a third and so on. If a contestant is not able to perform the actions in order, they are disqualified. The winner is the last person able to perform all the actions in order.

89 Blow ball

Divide the cell into two equal teams giving each team one table-tennis ball and each team member a straw.

Have the teams stand on one side of the room and place a chair per team on the opposite side of the room. The first member of each team goes on his knees and with the drinking straw propels the ball across the room and around the chair by blowing through the straw. When they return, the next person does the same until everybody has completed. The winning team is the first to finish the exercise.

90 Tasters

Ask a few volunteers from the group to leave the room. Set up a few beverages for tasting, eg mango juice, water, vinegar, lemonade, etc.

Bring back each contestant separately and blindfolded, assuring them that all the beverages are drinkable. Instruct them to take a sip of each beverage and try to identify it. The winner is the person who identifies the most beverages. Have some beverages that have similar tastes to create a bit of confusion.

91 Animal, vegetable or mineral

Played on the same principle as twenty questions, one contestant silently chooses an object and informs the rest of the cell which category it falls into: animal, vegetable or mineral. The rest of the cell then have to ask questions trying to identify the object. However, the questions can only be answered with a 'Yes' or 'No'. Only 'No' answers are counted as a question. An outright guess, eg 'Is it a banana?' is counted as a question. The player who correctly identifies the teaser has the opportunity to set the next teaser. If no one guesses correctly, the original player gets to select a second teaser.

92 Celebrity

Cut out a number of famous faces from magazines and paste them on a cardboard poster. Number your pictures. Stick the poster up on the wall and have the cell members guess who the characters are, writing down their answers correlating with the correct number. The winner is the person who correctly identifies the most people.

93 You're talking nonsense

You will need one piece of paper per cell member for this ice-breaker. Get each cell member to jot down a topic on their paper, anything from the sublime to the ridiculous. For example, 'Are chickens actually extraterrestrials?', 'What is it like to live inside a ping-pong ball?', etc.

The topics are collected and placed into a hat. Each cell member then gets to choose a piece of paper and has to talk for one or two minutes on the topic they have chosen.

When everybody has had a chance to speak, the winner is chosen by the rest of the cell by means of applause.

94 Appointments

Give everybody a few minutes to make three appointments — 3 pm, 6 pm and 9 pm. After that have everyone stand in a circle. When you shout, '3 pm', everybody meets their 3 pm appointment and finds out two or three things about the other. After a short while, shout, '6 pm' and '9 pm', and let them do the same as for the first appointment. After they have met with all three of their appointments, have some people share about those they met.

This game can be used as an introduction where people introduce others instead of themselves.

95 People bingo

Give each person attending the cell meeting a copy of the people bingo sheet.

Instruct them that at the word 'Go' they are to pair off with someone and ask them one question from the bingo list which they feel applies to that person and which the person will reply 'Yes' to. If the person that they asked responds 'Yes', they fill that person's name in in the block of that particular question. They may not fill in one person's name more than once.

They then move on to another person and repeat the procedure. The winner is the first person to fill a line, whether horizontal, vertical or diagonal. The first person to finish shouts 'ice-breaker!'

wears glasses	uses an electric razor	can whistle the national anthem	did not make their bed today	has black hair
enjoys love stories	still has tonsils	Is left handed	does not own a car	lies about age
has broken an arm	hates milk	has long nails	often cries at the movies	can do a hand-stand
has never changed a nappy	plays guitar	sings in the shower	is a new Christian	loves cabbage
has ridden a motor cycle	is a bad swimmer	enjoys watching sport	is wearing blue socks	studied at a university or college
has broken a window	has bunked school	can do twenty push-ups	owns an oil painting	has never flown overseas

96 Kidney transplant

Use this as a group discussion exercise.

Tonight, the board of review at a general hospital meets to consider applicants for kidney transplants.

Each of the patients described below has been evaluated by the medical staff and it has been determined that each patient will probably die in three to six weeks without a transplant. The best statistician estimates are that only about five donors will be available during that period.

The board must establish a priority list of who will get the kidneys by ranking in order the nine applicants.

1. John Hallbright. Age forty-one. Married. Two children, a son of twelve and a daughter of four. College graduate. Works in a bank. Wife also employed as a primary school teacher.

2. Marie Flynn. Age thirty-nine. Unmarried. College graduate. Holds a MSc in physiotherapy. Employed at a hospital for fourteen years. Head of physiotherapy and occupational therapy treatment centre.

3. Pamela Watson. Age twenty-three. Married, no children. College graduate. Teaches social studies at secondary school. Medical diagnosis indicates a heart condition that may cause complications in a transplant operation.

4. Alan Smith. Age fifty-one. Married. Three children, daughter of nineteen, sons of seventeen and fifteen. Owner and operator of Smith Industries, Inc., a machine shop that employs 150. Councillor for twelve years; member of library board of directors for six years.

5. William Work. Age eleven. One of seven children of Mr and Mrs Ralph Work. Has received a kidney transplant that failed.

6. Walker Red Cloud. Age twenty-two. At least four children by two wives. Basic education. No occupation.

7. Nancy Adams. Age thirty-four. Divorced. Three children, daughter of seven, twin sons of six, all in her custody.

Employed as a secretary at an estate agent's. Receives no child support from her ex-husband whose whereabouts are unknown.

8. Mary Parenti. Age twelve. IQ 87. Teachers describe her as shy, withdrawn and inhibited. Family emigrated to UK the year she was born. Family owns a restaurant where both parents work.

9. Juan Gonzalez. Age thirty-two. Married, eight children. Migrant worker. Wife and three oldest children also work as migrant workers.

97   Can you follow instructions?

A read and do test   **Time limit: three minutes**

1. Read all that follows before doing anything.
2. Write your name in the upper right-hand corner of this page.
3. Circle the word 'corner' in sentence two.
4. Draw five small squares in the upper left-hand corner of this page.
5. Put an 'X' on each square.
6. Put a circle around each square.
7. Sign your name under line five.
8. After your name write 'yes, yes, yes'.
9. Put a circle around number 7.
10. Put an 'X' on the lower left-hand corner of this page.
11. Draw a triangle around the 'X' you just made.
12. Call out your first name when you get to this point.
13. On the reverse side of this paper add 6950 and 9805.
14. Put a circle around your answer.
15. Now that you have finished reading carefully, do only number 1 and 2.

PLEASE BE QUIET AND WATCH THE OTHERS FOLLOW THE INSTRUCTIONS.

98 The drawbridge

Read the story below, then follow the instructions at the end of the story.

As he left for a visit to his outlying districts, the jealous baron warned his pretty wife: 'Do not leave the castle while I am gone, or I will punish you severely when I return!'

But as the hours passed, the young baroness grew lonely and despite her husband's warning, decided to visit her lover who lived in the countryside nearby.

The castle was located on an island in a wide, fast-flowing river, with a drawbridge linking the island and the land at the narrowest point of the river.

'Surely my husband will not return before dawn,' she thought and she ordered her servants to lower the drawbridge and leave it down until she returned.

After spending several pleasant hours with her lover, the baroness returned to the drawbridge, only to find it blocked by a madman wildly waving a long, cruel knife. 'Do not attempt to cross this bridge, baroness, or I will kill you,' he raved.

Fearing for her life, the baroness returned to her lover and asked him to help.

'Our relationship is only a romantic one,' he said. 'I will not help.'

The baroness then sought out a boatman on the river, explained her plight to him, and asked him to take her across the river in his boat.

'I will do it, but only if you can pay my fee of five marks.'

'But I have no money with me!' the baroness protested.

'That is too bad. No money, no ride,' the boatman said flatly.

Her fears growing, the baroness ran crying to the home of a friend and after explaining the situation, she begged for enough money to pay the boatman his fee.

'If you had not disobeyed your husband, this would not have happened,' the friend said. 'I will give you no money.'

With dawn approaching and her last resource exhausted, the baroness returned to the bridge in desperation, attempted to cross to the castle and was slain by the madman.

Directions

In the preceding story, there are six characters. They are (in alphabetical order):

The baron   _____

The baroness   _____

The boatman   _____

The friend   _____

The lover   _____

The madman   _____

Using the list above, rank each character according to how responsible he or she was for the baroness's death. Rank the characters from 1 – 6, with 1 being the most responsible and 6 being the least responsible. Now work with the other members of your group and decide as a group on a rank order for the six characters.

99 Lifeboat

Divide the cell into groups of four to five people and have them discuss the following scenario.

An ocean liner sinks at sea and seven people escape in a lifeboat. Unfortunately, the lifeboat only has enough room and supplies for five people. Therefore, two people will have to abandon the lifeboat. The ocean contains hungry sharks, so the people who leave the boat will die.

You must select two people who will have to be sacrificed. Justify the reasons why you picked these two and also justify why the five should live.

To help you make your selection, the following information is presented:

1. A one-year-old baby travelling with its grandmother. The baby is extremely sick, suffering from a rare disease, but possibly treatable.

2. The baby's fifty-five-year-old grandmother. She is in good health but has been depressed since the death of her husband.

3. The captain of the ocean liner. He is thirty-one years old and has six children. His wife is dead and he has no insurance.

4. A seventy-year-old scientist. He is one of the original developers of the atomic bomb which was dropped on Japan during World War Two. His recent research might possibly lead to the cure for lung cancer in the next year or two.

5. A forty-two-year-old pregnant woman. Gossip on the ship indicates that she may be a prostitute. Her heavy make-up and style of clothing seem to indicate that the gossip is true.

6. A twenty-one-year-old university student. He is a rugby player. He is extremely brilliant and has an IQ of 140. He is a homosexual and very active in gay rights.

7. A seventy-two-year-old doctor who is a specialist in rare childhood diseases. Some people think he is a saint, but

what most of the do not know is that he is a drug addict. The police are investigating him because there is evidence that he sells drugs to young people.

100 Bible mime

Divide the cell into teams of three to six people. Every team selects one biblical event to mime for the other teams who try to identify the Bible story being acted out.

101 Silent auction

In silence, jot down in the left-hand margin the amount you bid on each item. The total amount you can bid for *all* items cannot exceed £2,000.00. When you open the bids, write the winner's name in the right-hand column.

Bids		Winner
£_____	World cup football tickets for two	_____
£_____	Original Van Gough painting	_____
£_____	A holiday for two in Hawaii	_____
£_____	Season tickets to the opera	_____
£_____	A year free at a health spa	_____
£_____	A red MG convertible	_____
£_____	To be on the Oprah Winfrey Show	_____
£_____	A date with a supermodel (female/male)	_____
£_____	One deep real friendship	_____
£_____	Any job that I want	_____
£_____	Breakfast in bed for one year	_____
£_____	A family holiday in Disneyland	_____
£_____	A holiday cottage by the sea	_____
£_____	A flight in Concorde	_____
£_____	Latest and best hi-fi	_____
£_____	A laser face-lift	_____
£_____	No hassles for one year	_____
£_____	**Total**	

102 Scrambled eggs

Materials needed per group:

  String
* Cottonwool (two rolls per group)
* Four empty egg boxes
  One raw egg
* One empty box (or three shoe boxes)
* Old newspapers
* Sellotape (one roll per group)
  Scissors

Preparation:

Tie the string around the egg, then attach it to the ceiling so it hangs about 1½ metres above the ground.

Objective:

Divide the group into teams. Give each team the materials marked with ∗. The objective is for the team to construct something so that when the string is cut, the egg will fall into an egg box without breaking.

Time allowed: ten to fifteen minutes.

103 Chubby cheeks

Get three or four people to participate and give them each a packet of marshmallows. The object of the game is to see which person can get the most marshmallows into their mouth without chewing or swallowing. After each person has put a marshmallow in their mouth, get each one to say 'Chubby cheeks'.

104 Memory game

For this game you will need five participants. Send four of the participants into another room of the building with the fifth person remaining behind. The cell leader then reads an article from a book or a newspaper to the remaining person — something that is not too complicated or long. You may only read the article once so the first participant must listen and concentrate very carefully. Once the article has been read, a second participant returns from the other room and the first participant has to repeat the article to the second. Again, the article when recited back, may not be repeated. The second participant then recites the article to the third and so on until all five participants have had a turn to hear the article from the previous participant. The fifth participant has to recite the article to the entire group. At the end of the game, the cell leader reads the article to the group.

105 Call! One, two, three

This ice-breaker will work well with a group of people who do not know each other very well.

Arrange the cell in a circle and instruct them to learn the name of the person on either side. One person stands in the centre and slowly turns around. This player then points at someone and says, 'Call left, one, two, three.' Before the sentence is finished, the person pointed at must call out the name of the person on their left. If the centre person said, 'Call right, one, two, three', the indicated person would call out the name of the person on their right. A failure to supply their neighbour's name will result in them becoming the centre player. Change the positions of the players every now and then to add to the excitement. By the end of the game everyone will know the names of the other guests.

106 Forbidden words

Each cell member is given a number of counters (match sticks, beans, etc.). They then have to start talking to the other cell members, asking them questions. As soon as someone says the words 'Yes' or 'No', they have to forfeit a counter to the person they are conversing with. The cell member with the most counters at the end of the game is the winner.

107 Grey elephant in Denmark

1. Get your cell to pick a number between 2 and 9, eg 4.
2. Multiply that number by 9 (eg 4 x 9 = 36).
3. Everybody will have a two-digit number. They must then add these two numbers together, eg 3 + 6 = 9. It will always add up to 9.
4. They must now subtract 5 from that number, eg 9 — 5 = 4. It will always be 4.

5. Tell them now to take that number's corresponding letter, eg 1 = A, 2 = B, 3 = C, etc. It will always be 'D'. Ask them to think of a country beginning with that letter — don't give them too much time. Most people think of Denmark.

6. They must think of an animal starting with the second letter of that word. Most people think of an elephant.

7. They must now think of its colour — grey.

8. Astound them by saying that they are thinking of a 'grey elephant in Denmark'.

108 Personality quiz

Who is the mystery person? The cell leader chooses a number of personalities, ie actors/singers/politicians, etc.

The cell is divided into teams and points are awarded for the team that is able to identify the mystery person first.

For example:

1. The actor with the charming smile (five-point answer);
2. Married to Nicole (three-point answer);
3. Acted in *Top Gun* (one-point answer).

Answer: Tom Cruise.

109 Holy land quiz

This is a similar ice-breaker to the personality quiz, except that places in Israel are used.

For example:

1. A very important town according to property;
2. Joseph and Mary went from Nazareth to the town for a census;
3. Jesus was born there.

Answer: Bethlehem.

110 The gargle game

Give each person a mystery song. Allow each cell member to gargle their song. As soon as one of the cell members is able to identify the song they should shout 'Stop!' The person who identifies the most songs wins!

111 Tasting time

Choose three people from the cell to be involved in a tasting competition. Place before them five or six bowls of differently – flavoured potato crisps, eg tomato, salt and vinegar, barbecue.

They must attempt to correctly identify the flavour of each bowl. The winner is the person with the most correct guesses.

112 Straws and peas

A soup bowl filled with dried whole peas, a saucer for each player and a packet of peas are required. The bowl of peas is placed in the centre of the table. Each player is supplied with a straw with which they transfer as many peas as possible from the bowl onto their saucers by sucking them onto the end of the straw. If a pea is dropped on the table it must remain there, or be picked up on the end of the straw.

113 Tickle game

1. Arrange the group into pairs.
2. One is the tickler and the other the ticklee. The tickler has to attempt to make the ticklee laugh by using positive words, not fingers, to praise the ticklee. The ticklee must try to not laugh.
3. Swap roles once ticklee has laughed.

Discuss at the end why we laugh. Is it because it makes us uncomfortable to be praised? Share ideas and viewpoints about self-praise and accepting praise from others.

114   I hear the wind blow

Count the number of people in the group and get chairs for each person except one. One person stands in the middle of the circle and says, 'I hear the wind blow for ...'. Then he/she has to say something about themselves that everyone has or that at least two/three people in the group have. (Eg 'someone who has love in their heart', or 'someone who has brown hair', or 'someone with a right ear). Make it interesting! All the people in the group with those characteristics, including the one in the middle, have to run and find a chair. However, they are not allowed to take the chair next to them, it has to be at least two chairs away. The person who is left without a chair then has to stand in the middle and start the game again.

115   Blanket draw

Divide your cell into two teams. Nominate a leader in each team. Two neutral people hold up a blanket so that the two teams are unable to see one another.

The leader then decides who will represent the team in the first draw. These players face one another with the blanket separating them. On the word 'Go'. the blanket is dropped and the two facing each other must shout out the other person's name. The first to do so wins the draw. The loser joins the winner's team. Continue until one team is 'wiped out'.

116   English trap

Divide your cell into four groups. Rotate the following questions to each group and see how many each group answers correctly.

1. What word starts with 'is', ends with 'nd' and has 'la' in the middle.

Answer: Island.

2. What is one thing that all wise men, regardless of their religion or politics, agree is between heaven and earth?

Answer: The word 'and'.

3. What is at the beginning of eternity, the end of time, the beginning of every end, and the end of every place?

Answer: The letter 'E'.

4. There is a word in the English language in which the first two letters signify a male, the first three signify a female, the first four a great man, and the whole word, a great woman. What is the word?

Answer: Heroine (He, Her, Hero, Heroine).

5. Which word in the English language is always pronounced incorrectly?

Answer: Incorrectly.

117   Shadows

Give each member of your cell a blank piece of white paper and a pair of scissors. Ask each person to cut out a side view or silhouette of someone in the cell. Present the silhouettes one by one on a black sheet of paper, allowing the cell to guess who it is.

118   *Personal true or false*

Allow each person five minutes to list ten true and ten false statements about themselves. Give each person an opportunity to read his/her list, allowing the group to guess whether the statement is true or false.

The winner is the person who 'cons' the rest of the group the most number of times.

For example:

I have broken an arm;
I have jumped out of an aeroplane;
I am allergic to fish.

2
SERIOUS ICE-BREAKERS

Ten tips for serious ice-breakers

1. Preparation is the key to successful serious ice-breakers.
2. Spend time praying beforehand, so that the Holy Spirit will unlock your cell member's heart through this time.
3. Never allow a single person to dominate the discussion.
4. It is important that the leader shares first. This avoids the problem of light-hearted simplistic responses from cell members.
5. Be as real and as transparent as you can.
6. Listen to the person sharing and listen to the Holy Spirit.
7. Be gentle and caring.
8. Allow the serious ice-breaker to flow into a time of ministry if necessary.
9. Avoid trying to give answers.
10. Allow the love of Jesus to flow through you.

1 Collage

Divide everyone into groups of four (two cell members and two visitors).

Give each person:

1. At least two 'secular' magazines;
2. A4 blank white sheet of paper;
3. A pen or any colour pencil;
4. An envelope (with a stamp on it, if you can).

Give each group:

1. Two pairs of scissors;
2. One or two tubes of glue.

Give the following instructions:

1. Write your name and surname, postal address and telephone number on the back of the piece of paper.
2. You are about to use your creative talents by making a collage.

Using pictures and slogans any way you want, answer the following questions:

1. What has been the highlight of your year so far?
2. What has been the lowlight of your year so far?
3. What would you like to see happen in your family this year?
4. What would you like to see happen in your relationship with God?

Give everyone about twenty-five minutes to do this. Once they have finished, arrange the group into pairs (your organising now is vital — the last thing you want is for two non-Christian people to pair off). As the cell leader you must say who goes with whom.

Direct the group as follows:

1. In pairs, facing one another, discuss the questions and answers. (When you see the discussion is drawing to a close, encourage everyone to pray for their partner. Just a short prayer.)
2. Now swap collages with your partner.
3. Write your partner's name and address on the envelope.
4. For the next three days, pray for your partner, that God's will be done in their lives and that God will grant them the desires of their heart.
5. After three days, write a short letter of encouragement and post the letter and collage back to your partner.

2 Weather report

Go around the cell and let each person describe their week so far by means of a weather report, using weather terminology, eg. fine, mild, cloudy, stormy, gales, high or low pressures, etc. Explain why your week was so.

3 Incomplete Bible verses

Read Scripture portions, purposely omitting words which must be filled in by your cell.

Take most of the quotations from familiar verses, adding one or two more difficult ones for the Bible whizzes in your cell.

4 Scrambled verses

Have three or four verses written out on small pieces of paper. However, the verses must be scrambled as shown below.

The original verse:

'Therefore, if anyone is in Christ, he is a new creation, the old has gone, the new has come!' (2 Corinthians 5:17).

As scrambled and given to the cell:

'is in Christ, the old, if anyone, he is a new, the new, Therefore, has gone, creation; has come!'

Divide your cell into two or three teams and give each team the same verse. Instruct them to unscramble the verse, show you if it is correct, then find the reference in the Bible. As soon as the first team finds the correct reference, go to the next verse.

It might be advisable to use scriptures that you will be looking at in your edification time. Do not make the verses too long.

Award the winning team with a small prize for their effort.

5 Innovative introduction 1

Instruct the cell members to take out two personal items from their pockets, wallet, etc. Once they have them out, explain what they are to do with them.

Let them use these items to introduce themselves and share something about themselves.

6 Innovative introduction 2

Ask each cell member to state their name and attach an adjective that not only describes a dominant characteristic, but also starts with the first letter of their name, eg Shy Sharon, Boisterous Barry, Funny Frank, etc.

7 Innovative introduction 3

Have each cell member share a nickname that they now have or have had and let them explain how they acquired that nickname.

8 How are you feeling?

Give every cell member a blank piece of paper. Flash the following words written on a big piece of paper.

ANXIETY	**FORGIVENESS**	**GUILT**
SORROW	**HEALING**	**REJECTION**
PEACE	**PAIN**	**COMFORT**
LOVE	**ACCEPTANCE**	**HOPE**

Ask everyone to write down on their piece of paper the word that describes how they are feeling or what they want Jesus to bring them now. Place all the papers in the centre of the group and mix them up well. Choose a piece of paper from the pile and read out aloud what is written on it. Have a time for people to share a phrase or verse which might encourage the person whose paper has been picked. Do as many papers as you can in the time.

9 Animal feelings

Ask the cell, 'If you have to pick an animal below to describe how this cell has reshaped your life, what would you pick?'

1. Colourful peacock
Because you have told me that I am beautiful and I have started to believe it and it is changing my life.

2. Lovable hippopotamus
Because you have let me surface and bask in the warm sunshine of God's love.

3. Leopard
Because you have have helped me look very closely at myself and see some of the spots ... and you have told me it's OK to be this way.

4. Dancing bear
Because you have taught me to dance in the midst of pain and you have helped me to reach out and hug again.

5. Roaring lion
Because you have let me get down off my perch and roll in the grass and not even worry about my mane.

6. Wild eagle
Because you have helped to heal my wings and taught me how to soar again.

7. Towering giraffe
Because you have helped me to hold my head up high and stick my neck out.

8. All-weather duck
Because you have taught me to enjoy the weather (even on

rainy days) and to celebrate the hard times like a duck in a storm.

9. Ostrich in love

Because you have loved me so much that I have taken my head out of the sand and found a whole new reason for living.

10 Personal inventory

Take a moment and make an inventory of your own life. Bob Munger, in his little booklet *'My Heart — Christ's Home'*, described the areas of one's life as rooms in a house. Give yourself a grade on each room as follows: A = excellent rating; B = good rating; C = passable, but needs a little dusting, and D = barely pass, needs a lot of cleaning.

☐ *Study*
This room is your mind. What you allow to go into and come out of it. It is the 'control room' of the entire house.

☐ *Dining room*
Appetites, desires, those things on which your mind and spirit feed for nourishment.

☐ *Bedroom*
This is where you draw close to God and seek time with him daily, not just in times of distress and need.

☐ *Toolshed*
This room is where your gifts, talents and skills are put to work for God ... by the power of the Spirit.

☐ *Lounge*
The social area of your life; the things you do to amuse yourself and others.

☐ *Understairs cupboard*
The one secret place that no one knows about, but which is a real stumbling block in your walk in the Spirit.

Questions to generate discussions in your cell

11 Ice-breaker

Let the cell members each share on:

1. Their first real job;
2. Their first real salary;
3. How they got to work each day.

12 Ice-breaker

Let everyone share what they will be doing for Christmas. (Cell leaders: be sensitive as to who will be alone, and see if you can help in any way. Do not discuss the solution in the cell meeting, putting them on the spot or making them feel uncomfortable.)

13 Ice-breaker

As people arrive, collect one item from each person, eg a watch, earring, wallet, sock, etc., and put them into a bag.
- Ask each person to take one item from your bag (not their own).
- Each person must then guess whose item they have.
- Get into pairs and pray for each other.

14 Ice-breaker

- Which one thing would you change about your family right now.

15 Ice-breaker

- If your friend lent you his or her shirt and you ruined it — but you could replace it without your friend finding out, what would you do? Why?

16 Ice-breaker

- Let people share what characteristic or personality trait they see in the person on their left, which they desire for their own life. As the cell leader, start this off but *do not* make it too serious — this must be light-hearted but truthful. Use your initiative in making this enjoyable and not sombre.

17 Ice-breaker

- Ask members to share any good, clean jokes they have recently heard.
- What was the most significant thing that happened to you during the week?

18 Ice-breaker

- Ask the group, 'Which is your favourite advert on TV?' Get some of them to act out their most irritating advert, accents and all.
- 'Do you ever actually shop for the things you see advertised on TV?'
- 'What would you do with the money if you won a million pounds?'

19 Ice-breaker

- Try and describe to each other what happens to the value system of a person who falls head-over-heels in love.
- Share with the group what happened to you when you fell in love.

20 Ice-breaker

- Would you like to tell us about the most difficult situation you have ever been in? (As the cell leader, it would be advisable for you to start sharing first.)

- What is the most outstanding answer to prayer that you have ever experienced?

21 Ice-breaker

- What is the most amazing physical thing you have ever seen a person do?
- Have you ever seen a miracle? Share brief details.
- Have you ever heard of a person being raised from the dead?

22 Ice-breaker

- If you could prophesy a positive future over Britain, what would you like to include in your prophecy? What things would you like to take place in our land?
- Have you ever had anyone prophesy over you? Are there any parts of the prophecy which you would feel comfortable to share with the cell group?

23 Ice-breaker

- What is the best thing that has happened to you this year so far?
- If you could choose two great things that could happen to you before the end of the year, what would you choose?

24 Ice-breaker

Place a jug filled with water in the centre of the room. Place an empty glass in a basin or on a large plate and say, 'Will someone please fill the glass with water to illustrate how full God wants each of us to be filled with the Holy Spirit.'

Ask anyone to fill the glass again to the highest level to which they have ever been filled with the Holy Spirit. Ask the question: 'How does one get fuller?'

25 Ice-breaker

- When did you first hear about the Holy Spirit?
- What was your reaction the first time you saw the gifts of the Spirit in operation?
- When, for the first time, did you understand what speaking in tongues was all about?

26 Ice-breaker

- If your boss offered you a pay rise but you knew that you did not deserve it, would you accept it?

27 Ice-breaker

- If you could ask God one question, what would it be?

28 Ice-breaker

- Which is worse: spreading rumours you know are not true or saying a true but unkind thing to someone face to face?

29 Ice-breaker

- What is your favourite day of the week? Why?

30 Ice-breaker

- When was the last time you really felt hurt? Share with the rest of the cell about it.

31 Ice-breaker

- Do you act differently around church people than you do around other people? Explain.

32 Ice-breaker

- Is it more important for you to be with Christian friends or non-Christian friends? Explain.

33 Ice-breaker

- Which is worse: a teenager cheating in a test or a parent making unauthorised, personal, long-distance calls on the company telephone?

34 Ice-breaker

- When did you first believe in Jesus? How did that change your relationships with other people?

35 Ice-breaker

- Who are the two people who you can truly say loved/loves you? How did they show their love for you?

36 Ice-breaker

Discuss around the room (everyone to participate):
- When was the last time the Lord communicated with you?
- How does the Lord communicate with you?

37 Ice-breaker

- When was the last time you did something for the first time?

38 Ice-breaker

- If you could live in any country in the world, where would you choose to settle and why?

39 Ice-breaker

- When was the last time you had to stay focussed, persevere, concentrate and not be moved? Share the details with the group.

40 Ice-breaker

1. Who has been the person who has had a major influence on your life up till now? Why do you say so?
2. Who do you go to for spiritual counsel? Why?

41 Ice-breaker

Hand out a slip of paper to each person. Each piece of paper has a topic on it, eg:

1. My future
2. My purpose in life
3. My life thus far
4. Reaching the lost
5. My role at church
6. Money
7. Christians
8. Temptation

Do not let them look at the topic until you say so. As the person turns the piece of paper over, have them share their *immediate* thoughts on the topic as it relates to their *own* life. Keep it short and sweet. *No DEBATING!*

42 Ice-breaker

- When have you seen that it is more blessed to give than to receive?

43 Ice-breaker

Divide into groups of four and answer the following questions:

1. What is the favourite room in your house? Why?
2. If you had a major decision to make and you were confused as to what to decide, to whom would you go to for advice and why?

44 Ice-breaker

- What did Jesus say about the kingdom of God in the 'Lord's Prayer', and what did he mean?

45 Ice-breaker

1. In your childhood years, who helped raise you? Who helped with your nappies? Fed You? Helped you with your homework? Bathed you? etc. Why?
2. Who was your favourite teacher at school? Why?

46 Ice-breaker

- Who is the most powerful person you know? How or why are they powerful — strength, money, emotional, spiritual, etc?

47 Ice-breaker

- Share with the group the story behind the longest time that you went without sleep.

48 Ice-breaker

1. Who influenced, encouraged or helped you choose your field of work or hobby that you have?
2. Is this your heart's desire? Why? If not, what is?

Pray for one another for fulfilment and purpose in life.

49 Ice-breaker

- What characteristic or personality trait do you see in the lives of other Christians which you really desire to see in your own life? Why?

50 Ice-breaker

- Share with the group how you came to know the Lord and who was most instrumental in leading you to Christ.

51 Ice-breaker

- If you could take a two-week free trip to any place in the world, where would it be?

52 Ice-breaker

- If you could become the leader of any country in the world, which would it be and why?

53 Ice-breaker

- If you could travel on a time machine to any era in time, which would it be and why?

54 Ice-breaker

- If you could talk to any person now living, who would it be?

55 Ice-breaker

- Explain a situation in your own life in which you tried to accomplish a God-given task through your own strength and could not do it.

56 Ice-breaker

- Give the cell a few minutes to search the room in which you are, to find something that they feel describes themselves, eg a flower — full of the fragrance of God; a book — studious, or a vase — fragile and delicate.
- Do the rest of the group agree with their description?

57 Ice-breaker

- Give an incident in your life where you made a decision which had life-changing implications. (Apart from your salvation experience.)

58 Ice-breaker

- Are you a creature of habit, comfortable with the familiar, or do you like to take risks?
- How do you break habits you should not have?

59 Ice-breaker

- As you have been growing up, has the law had a purpose in your life or has it hurt you?
- As a child, were you afraid of authority figures? If so, why?

60 Ice-breaker

- Has God blessed you lately? If so, in what way?

61 Ice-breaker

- Do you have a hobby? If so, what is it?
- If you really want to relax, what do you do?

62 Ice-breaker

- As a child in your home, were you given jobs for which you were responsible?
- Would you say that you are a responsible person?

63 Ice-breaker

- Where do you usually go for holidays?
- If money was no object, where would you go for your next holiday and why?

64 Ice-breaker

- Would you say you are a confident person.
- Do you find it easy to address a crowd or are you more a one-to-one person?

65 Ice-breaker

- What role does the Holy Spirit play in your life?

66 Ice-breaker

- Share some of the promises that God has given to you for your life.
- What are some of the things he wants to do through you?

67 Ice-breaker

- What has been the highlight of your cell meetings this year so far?

68 Ice-breaker

- What is the single most important thing that has happened to you since we last met?
- Share a specific answer to prayer you experienced during this time.

69 Ice-breaker

- Share how someone reached out to you when you were in a time of need and nobody knew about it.
- What were the results of you reaching out to somebody last week?

70 Ice-breaker

- Give the cell a short scripture that they must memorise for the following week's cell meeting.

71 Ice-breaker

- What was your happiest moment this past week?
- How has your concept of happiness changed over the years as you were growing up?

72 Ice-breaker

- If your house was on fire, which three items would you try and save? Why these particular items?

73 Ice-breaker

- Who is the easiest and most difficult person for you to forgive?

  a) brother/sister
  b) neighbour/friend
  c) spouse
  d) stranger
  e) parents/kids
  f) yourself.

- What does Jesus say about forgiveness in the Lord's Prayer (Matthew 6:9)? Pray for your cell members if necessary.

74 Ice-breaker

- How tidy did you keep your room or cupboard at home?
- Have your habits changed or improved with age?

75 Ice-breaker

- How important do you consider 'being on time' to be?
- Share with one another the most embarrassing moment that occurred when you were late.
- What do you think people think of your character or integrity when you always arrive late?

76 Ice-breaker

- How would you pass God's forgiveness to those who have wronged you?
  a) pray for them;
  b) think first about whether I have done anything wrong;
  c) drop the issue and let them know that it is past history;
  d) look for ways to show kindness to them.

77 Ice-breaker

- 'Seek first his kingdom.' What does this mean?
  a) get rid of your Merc/BMW;
  b) put God first and keep your Merc/BMW;
  c) check it out with God;
  d) establish your priorities.
- What are your priorities in life?

78 Ice-breaker

- What rules did your family have that you, as a kid, thought were stupid?
- How do you view those rules now?

79 Ice-breaker

- If you could be free of just one thing, what would it be?
- Read Luke 8:22-25.
- This ice-breaker could lead into a time of ministry as the Spirit leads.

80 Ice-breaker

- What do you do when people come to you in a shop or on the street and ask for money?
  a) ignore them;
  b) give them money without asking questions;
  c) assume you are being conned;
  d) share the gospel with them and pray;
  e) take them to the pastor because he is better equipped to handle them.
- Why is this your response?
- Read Luke 10:25-37.

81 Ice-breaker

- When you were at school, who was your biggest rival in academics, sport and social gatherings?
- Why did they have this impact on you?

82 Ice-breaker

- When was your most recent 'mountain-top' experience with God (Mark 9:2)?
- Share some detail of the experience.

83 Ice-breaker

- If you brought three dirty, homeless people home for Christmas lunch, how do you think your family would react?

84 Ice-breaker

- Ephesians 6:2-3 says, 'Honour your father and mother ... that you may enjoy long life on the earth.' According to this, how long do you think you'll live? Why?

85 Ice-breaker

- If you could always drive 20 mph over the speed limit and never get caught, would you? Why or why not?

86 Ice-breaker

- Describe where you think you will be and what you will be doing in ten years time.

87 Ice-breaker

- Should you date people you wouldn't consider marrying?

88 Ice-breaker

- Imagine your pastor just delivered the worst sermon you had ever heard. On your way out of the church the pastor asks, 'How did you like my sermon?' What would you say?

89 Ice-breaker

- What is one family tradition you never want to give up? Why?
- What is one tradition you could live without? Why?

90 Ice-breaker

- If you could tell people when and how they were going to die, would you tell them?
- Would you want to know when and how you will die? Why or why not?

91 Ice-breaker

- Why does God allow tragedies to happen?

92 Ice-breaker

- When does a person become an adult? Explain your answer.

93 Ice-breaker

- What would you say to a friend if he/she had just had a bad haircut?

94 Ice-breaker

- If you didn't have to work for a living, what would you want to do? Why?

95 Ice-breaker

- If a co-worker asked you to cover for him/her so that the boss would not get cross, would you do it? Why or why not?

96 Ice-breaker

- If you could spend twenty-four hours with anyone in the world, who would it be?
- What would you do together?

97 Ice-breaker

- Why do you suppose God asks us to save sex for marriage?

98 Ice-breaker

- If you could end all wars by killing one innocent person, would you do it? Why or why not?
- What if that person was your best friend?
- What if that person was your worst enemy?

99 Ice-breaker

- If you knew Jesus would return tomorrow, what would you do today?

100 Ice-breaker

- If you were the judge in a drunk driving case involving a death, what punishment would you give the convicted drunk driver? Why?

101 Ice-breaker

- If you could relive any one day of your life, which day would it be?

102 Ice-breaker

- How would your life be different if God didn't exist?

103 Ice-breaker

- If a cashier gave you £5 too much change, what would you do?

104 Ice-breaker

- If ten people praise you and one criticises you, which comment do you think about the most?

105 Ice-breaker

- When you get to heaven, for what personal qualities will the angels applaud you?

106 Ice-breaker

- Which is worse: telling a white lie or hurting someone's feelings? Why?

107 Ice-breaker

- If you could be launched 2,000 years into the future or 2,000 years into the past, which would you choose? Why?

108 Ice-breaker

- If a good friend had bad breath, what would you do?

109 Ice-breaker

- If you had been present at Jesus' crucifixion, what would you have done?

110 Ice-breaker

- Is it currently too easy to get a divorce? Explain.

111 Ice-breaker

- If you were driving along and to avoid an accident, you had to hit a cat or a wall with your brand-new car, which would you choose? Why?

112 Ice-breaker

- Do you think God would send a disease like AIDS to punish homosexuals and drug-users? Why or why not?

113 Ice-breaker

- Will people who have never heard of Jesus Christ go to hell? Explain.

114 Ice-breaker

- How do you know what true love is?

115 Ice-breaker

- Is it easier for you to give or receive compliments? Why?

116 Ice-breaker

- Have you ever popped a grape or strawberry into your mouth in a supermarket without paying for it?
- Is that stealing?
- Would Jesus do that? Why or why not?

117 Ice-breaker

- If your friends knew everything about you, would they still be your friends? Explain.

118 Ice-breaker

- Do you like your name?
- If you could, to what would you change your name?

119 Ice-breaker

- In what ways are you a different parent to your own parents?

120 Ice-breaker

- If you had a vivid dream three nights in a row in which God asked you to leave everything and become a missionary in a tiny far-off village, would you do it? Why or why not?

121 Ice-breaker

- Is there someone you now like, but didn't like when you first met him or her? Why?

122 Ice-breaker

- If a reporter on national television asked you to describe the best thing about your cell group, what would you say?

123 Ice-breaker

- How does a person get to heaven?

124 Ice-breaker

- What is your biggest worry? Why?

125 Ice-breaker

- Imagine you were in a packed cinema. What would you do if a total stranger next to you talked throughout the film?

126 Ice-breaker

- What do you think a messy bedroom says about the person who lives in it?

127 Ice-breaker

- Should your children obey you even if you knew you were wrong?

128 Ice-breaker

- If you could read someone's mind, whose would it be? Why?

129 Ice-breaker

- If you knew that eating health foods and cutting out such foods as hamburgers would add ten years to your life, would you do it? Why or why not?

130 Ice-breaker

- Would you lie in a job application if you knew you wouldn't be caught? Explain.

131 Ice-breaker

- Suppose your best friend occasionally used the Lord's name in vain. What would you do?

132 Ice-breaker

- Does money buy happiness? Explain.

133 Ice-breaker

- If you knew someone had been gossiping about you, would you confront them? Why or why not?

134 Ice-breaker

- If a family member didn't want to take a phone call and asked you to say that they were out, what would you do?
- Which Christian principles apply here?

135 Ice-breaker

- Does God have a sense of humour? Explain.

136 Ice-breaker

- Which is the easier to raise, a boy or a girl? Why?

137 Ice-breaker

- Is your house too tidy or too messy? Explain.

138 Ice-breaker

- If your life flashed before your eyes, which moment would you not want to see?

139 Ice-breaker

- Are there ever any really good reasons to commit suicide?

140 Ice-breaker

- Which household appliance are you the most like? Explain.

141 Ice-breaker

- What is the most stupid thing you have ever done on a dare?

142 Ice-breaker

- If you could have only one of five senses, which would it be? Why?

143 Ice-breaker

- If your neighbour's dog 'fertilises' your lawn, are you justified in tossing the droppings onto his/her lawn? Explain.

144 Ice-breaker

- What would you do if you saw a restaurant cook sneeze into a bowl of soup that was served to the table next to you?

145 Ice-breaker

- Would you date someone with a bad reputation? Why or why not?

146 Ice-breaker

- If Jesus was visiting our church, what would he think?

147 Ice-breaker

- Which interests you the most: the past, the present or the future? Why?

148 Ice-breaker

- Would you ever lie about how much you weigh or how old you are? Why?

Statements and scriptures to generate discussions in your cell

149 Ice-breaker

- A marriage may be made in heaven, but the maintenance must be done on earth (Ephesians 5:3).

150 Ice-breaker

- When God measures someone, he puts the tape around their heart instead of their head (1 Samuel 16:7b).

151 Ice-breaker

- Patience is the ability to keep the motor idling when you feel like stripping your gears (Proverbs 16:32).

152 Ice-breaker

- Many a good person has failed because they had their wishbone where their backbone should have been (Joshua 1:9).

153 Ice-breaker

- It's good to be a Christian and know it, but it's better to be a Christian and show it (John 13:35).

154 Ice-breaker

- Your companions are like the buttons on a lift. They will either take you up or they will take you down (Proverbs 13:20).

155 Ice-breaker

- Too many church-goers are singing, 'Standing on the promises' when all they are doing is sitting on the premises (Hebrews 6:12).

156 Ice-breaker

- The mighty oak was once a nut that stood its ground (Proverbs 12:3).

157 Ice-breaker

- Most people wish to serve God — but only in an advisory capacity (1 Peter 5:6).

158 Ice-breaker

- If you don't stand for something, you'll fall for anything (Isaiah 7:9b, NIV).

159 Ice-breaker

- The best way to forget your own problems is to help someone solve theirs (Philippians 2:4).

160 Ice-breaker

- God can heal a broken heart, but He has to have all the pieces (Proverbs 23:26a).

161 Ice-breaker

- The best way to get the last word is to apologise (Proverbs 6:2-3, NIV).

162 Ice-breaker

- When confronted with a Goliath-sized problem, which way do you respond 'He's too big to hit' or, like David, 'He's too big to miss' (1 Samuel 17:37)?

163 Ice-breaker

- No one ever said on their deathbed: 'I wish I had spent more time at work' (Ecclesiastes 2:18).

164 Ice-breaker

- You can't take your money with you, but you can send it on ahead (Matthew 6:19-20).

165 Ice-breaker

- Ability will enable a person to go to the top, but it takes character to keep them there (Proverbs 11:5, NIV).

166 Ice-breaker

- God plus one is always a majority (Romans 8:31b).

167 Ice-breaker

- Whoever gossips to you will gossip of you (Proverbs 11:13).

168 Ice-breaker

- Don't be afraid of pressure. Remember that pressure is what turns a lump of coal into a diamond (James 1:3-4).

169 Ice-breaker

- Reputation is made in a moment: character is built in a lifetime (Job 27:6).

170 Ice-breaker

- Take care of your character and your reputation will take care of itself (1 Timothy 4:8).

171 Ice-breaker

- The poorest of all people is not the person without a penny but the person without a dream (Proverbs 29:18a).

172 Ice-breaker

- To forgive is to set a prisoner free and discover the prisoner was YOU (Matthew 6:14-15).

173 Ice-breaker

- The best inheritance parents can leave their children is a good example (1 Thessalonians 2:11).

174 Ice-breaker

- True faith and courage are like a kite — an opposing wind raises it higher (Isaiah 40:31).

175 Ice-breaker

- The doors of opportunity are marked 'Push' and 'Pull' (Proverbs 13:4).

176 Ice-breaker

- A shut mouth gathers no food (Proverbs 13:3).

177 Ice-breaker

- Your words are windows to your heart (Matthew 12:34b).

178 Ice-breaker

- Pick your friends, but not to pieces (Proverbs 25:18).

179 Ice-breaker

- He who throws dirt loses ground (Ephesians 4:25).

180 Ice-breaker

- It is good to remember that the tea kettle, although up to its neck in hot water, continues to sing (1 Thessalonians 5:16, 18).

181 Ice-breaker

- Life can only be understood by looking backwards, but it must be lived by looking forwards (Luke 9:62).

182 Ice-breaker

- Falling down doesn't make you a failure, but staying down does (Proverbs 24:16a).

3
CELL OUTREACH EVENTS

Ten tips for cell outreach events

1. Make sure that you discuss and plan the outreach evening with your cell the week before:
   a) Who is to bring what;
   b) Inviting non-Christian friends;
   c) How to treat visitors.
2. Visitors are your top priority. Make them feel welcome, at home and important.
3. Whatever you do, do it with excellence. Remember, perfection is law, excellence is grace.
4. Put certain cell members in charge of hosting your visitors for the evening.
5. Prepare a fun ice-breaker that will allow everybody to get involved and get to know one another.
6. Avoid Christian jargon and cliques.
7. Be real!
8. Make a point of getting to know all your visitors; try to spend some time chatting to each one individually.
9. Share a bit about your cell near the end of the evening.
10. Invite the visitors back next week.

1 Pizza and pictionary party

This is a great way for reaching out to friends in a non-threatening and fun way.

Suggestions

1. Send out invitations through your cell members, on cards cut out to look like pizzas, to the people you are reaching out to.

2. Give each cell member two to three invitations and encourage them to invite their friends.
3. Ask each cell member to bring a pizza and a cold drink to the outreach evening.

On the evening

1. Have pleasant background music playing.
2. As cell members and visitors arrive, put the pizzas into a warm oven.
3. Welcome each person and offer them something to drink.
4. Use Pictionary at the beginning of the evening to break down inhibitions and to create a fun-filled atmosphere.
5. From the Pictionary, lead into supper, coffee and a good 'getting to know one another' chat.
6. Have a couple of cell members organise fun things like skits, a song or even a dance involving everybody.

Pictionary

1. When everybody has arrived, draw partners out of a hat and enjoy a game of Pictionary together.
2. Avoid putting couples together.

2 Junk-food crawl

Suggestions

1. Send out invitations on crumpled and greased brown paper bags or something similar.
2. Get your cell members to invite their friends.

Preparation

1. Organise enough vehicles to have transport for everyone.
2. Inform the people to bring whatever amount of money is needed for the evening.
3. Have a couple of cell members organise fun things like skits, a song or even a dance involving everybody.

On the evening

1. Meet at a central venue.
2. The course of the evening will take you to three or four fast-food restaurants where you will be having different meals, eg, you will have a starter at the first restaurant, your main meal at the second restaurant, your dessert at the third restaurant and coffee at the fourth restaurant.

3 Create a pizza evening

Suggestions

1. Send out invitations in the shape of a pizza.
2. On the invitation, request which ingredient must be brought on the evening. This would be any ingredient that is suitable as a topping for a pizza.
3. Get your cell members to invite their friends.

Preparation

1. It would be advisable to have this event at a venue with a lot of space and with more than one oven for cooking the pizzas.
2. Buy ready-made pizza bases.
3. Have enough bowls and containers in which to put the pizza topping ingredients.
4. Have all your ingredients on a table on one side of the room. Depending on the size of the group, you may need to lay out two separate tables of ingredients.
5. Have a couple of cell members organise fun things like skits, a song or even a dance involving everybody.

On the evening

1. Have pleasant background music playing to create an atmosphere.
2. Welcome all the guests.
3. Ask everybody to divide into groups of three or four, with people they do not know, give them each a pizza base and instruct them to create their own pizza.
4. Have a few ice-breakers prepared.

4 Kitsch and common party

Suggestions

1. If the evening is held in a hall, decorate it in line with the theme of the evening, eg pink flowers in a red vase, yellow tablecloths with red overlays, etc. Anything that does not match.
2. Get each cell member to invite a friend.
3. People must dress for the occasion — kitsch or common.
4. Ask each cell member to bring a plate of refreshments decorated in the theme, eg a green cake with bright pink icing.

On the evening

1. Have pleasant background music playing.
2. Welcome each person and offer them something to drink.
3. Have a prize for the best-dressed person. Pick out four or five of the best-dressed people and have them parade for everyone else. Their applause and cheers will determine the winning person.
4. Have a few ice-breakers prepared.
5. Have a couple of cell members organise fun things like skits, a song or even a dance involving everybody.

5 Mad-hatters tea party

Suggestions

1. Send out written invitations on cards in the shape of a teapot.
2. Give each cell member two or three invitations and encourage them to invite their friends.
3. Ask each cell member to bring a plate of refreshments suitable for a tea party, eg scones, biscuits, etc.
4. Remind everyone that they must wear an unusual head-dress for the party.

Preparation

1. Have the tea party outside in a garden.
2. Prepare and decorate a few tables with chairs around them.
3. Have a couple of cell members organise fun things like skits, a song or even a dance involving everybody.

On the day

1. Choose three or four people with the most original head-dress and have them parade for the group. The group's applause and cheers will decide the winning head-dress. Have a prize for that person.
2. Play a game of musical chairs.

6 Music knowledge quiz

Suggestions

1. Send out invitations on music sheets.
2. Give each cell member two or three invitations and encourage them to invite their friends.
3. Ask each cell member to bring a plate of refreshments.

Preparation

1. Record three or four second clips of songs onto a cassette. Mix your selection of songs with both old and new.
2. Prepare your questions beforehand with topics such as:
   a) Title of songs;
   b) Artist's or group's name;
   c) From which movie, if applicable;
   d) From which TV advertisement, if applicable.
3. Have different sections in the quiz:
   a) Individual team questions;
   b) Open team questions: where each team has an instrument (eg a bell, a horn, a whistle, a buzzer, etc.) to announce their participation in that question. The first sound heard gets to answer the question.
   c) Time limit team questions: how many questions can be answered by a particular team in an allotted time?
4. Allocate points per section, eg five points for a correct answer, minus five for an incorrect answer, three points if an incorrect answer is passed on and answered correctly by another team, or minus three if answered incorrectly, etc.

On the evening

1. Divide the group into teams. Eight people per team is normally a good size.
2. Have a board where the scores can be recorded.
3. Award extra points on certain questions where, if a participant has answered correctly, they must sing a portion of the song.

7 Fondue evening

A well-planned fondue evening always goes down very well with everybody.

Suggestions

1. Divide the ingredients that need to be brought among the cell members and ask everyone to bring a cool drink and a chocolate bar.

2. Encourage your cell members to invite friends that they are reaching out to.

Preparation

1. You will need one fondue pot per three or four people with two forks per person.
2. Arrange the fondue pots in a creative way around the room — a good idea is to put a blanket down on the floor with the fondue pot on a low table. Scatter a few cushions around it and create the atmosphere by lighting some candles.
3. Ingredients you can use are chopped up:
   a) beef
   b) pork
   c) mushrooms.
   d) chicken
   e) cherries wrapped in bacon
4. Organise a salad and a couple of garlic breads.

On the evening

1. Have light music playing in the background which helps to create a relaxing atmosphere.
2. As the guests arrive with the ingredients, divide them equally among the number of pots you have.
3. Avoid too much moving around. This can become dangerous with the fire under the pots.
4. For dessert, melt the chocolate bars with a bit of milk and dip marshmallows into it.

8 Black and white evening

Suggestions

1. Send out invitations on bow-tie shaped cards.
2. Give each cell member two or three invitations and encourage them to invite their friends.
3. Inform people on the invitation that the dress is strictly black and white — no other colours — even as far as make-up is concerned.
4. Ask each cell member to bring a plate of refreshments.

Preparation

1. Decorate the hall completely in black and white.
2. Have a couple of cell members organise fun things like skits, a song or even a dance involving everybody.

On the evening

1. Have pleasant background music playing to create an atmosphere.
2. Have a prize for the best-dressed person.
3. Have a few ice-breakers prepared.

9 Alphabet party

Suggestions

1. Send out invitations with the word 'Alphabet Party' on the front made up of letters cut out from newspapers.
2. Give each cell member two or three invitations and encourage them to invite their friends.
3. Inform the people that they are to come dressed up as anyone beginning with the first letter of their name. For example, if their name is Mandy, they could come as a mechanic, if their name is Stephen, they could come as a soldier, etc.
4. Ask each cell member to bring a plate of refreshments.

Preparation

1. Decorate the venue with anything to do with the alphabet, eg posters, large alphabetical letters, etc.

2. Have a couple of cell members organise fun things like skits, a song or even a dance involving everybody.

On the evening

1. Have light background music playing to create a fun atmosphere.
2. Have prizes for the best-dressed people.
3. Have a couple of large crowd ice-breakers prepared.

10 Disney evening

Suggestions

1. Send out invitations with Disney characters pasted on them.
2. Give your cell members two or three invitations and encourage them to invite their friends.
3. Inform people to dress as a Disney character.
4. Ask each cell member to bring a plate of refreshments.

Preparations

1. Decorate the venue in Disney style, ie posters, polystyrene Disney characters, etc.
2. Have a couple of cell members organise fun things like skits, a song or even a dance involving everybody.

On the evening

1. Have Disney music playing in the background.
2. Have a prize for the most authentically dressed person.
3. Have a couple of ice-breakers prepared.

11 Formal masked ball

Suggestions

1. Send out invitations on mask-shaped cards.
2. Give your cell member two or three invitations and encourage them to invite their friends.
3. On the invitation inform your guests that the dress is very formal and masks are essential.
4. Being a formal evening, it might be advisable to have a sit-down dinner. Therefore organise for someone to do the catering for the evening and charge a fee for the meal.

Preparations

1. Decorate the hall in the theme of a masked ball.
2. Set out and decorate the tables for a formal dinner.
3. Organise waiters and waitresses from another cell to assist you with serving for the evening.
4. Have a couple of cell members organise fun things like skits, a song or even a dance involving everybody.

On the evening

1. Have appropriate music for the evening, eg Phantom of the Opera, classical music, etc.
2. Have a competition and a prize for the best-dressed people, etc.

12 Hebrew dinner

Suggestions

1. Send out invitations with a Hebrew theme to them.
2. Give each cell member two or three invitations and encourage them to invite their friends that they are reaching out to.

3. On the invitation, stipulate the dress is Hebrew.
4. To make the evening a success, delegate certain tasks to cell members.
5. Organise that each cell member brings a plate of refreshments.

Preparations

1. Decorate the venue in a Hebrew theme, eg Hebrew candle-holders, etc.
2. Have a couple of cell members organise fun things like skits, a song or even a dance to Hebrew music involving everybody.

On the evening

1. Have Hebrew music playing in the background.
2. Welcome all your guests.
3. Take time to speak to the visitors.
4. Have a prize for the most authentically dressed person.

13 Beggar party

This party will work well for early evening. Make the venue a place that is visible to passers-by, and look at their expressions during the evening.

Suggestions

1. Send out invitations on crumpled and greased brown paper bags or something similar.
2. On the invitation, stipulate that people are to dress like beggars or tramps.

3. Give each cell member two or three invitations and encourage them to invite their friends.

Preparations

1. Buy all the food beforehand. The type of food that you can use is loaves of bread, french fries, milk, etc.
2. On the invitation, inform your guests of the cost of the evening (to cover the cost of the food which you must supply).

On the evening

1. Have everyone meet at a central venue. Don't let them know where they are going. Once they have all arrived, climb into your cars and take them off to the venue.
2. Sit on the floor around your food and enjoy the chance to throw away your inhibitions.

14 Hawaiian evening

This is one of the easiest evenings to organise in terms of decor, etc.

Suggestions

1. Send out invitations with a Hawaiian theme — eg palm trees, beaches.
2. Encourage cell members to invite their friends that they are reaching out to.
3. Ask each cell member to bring a plate of refreshments and organise ice-cream for dessert.

Preparations

1. Decorate the venue with a Hawaiian theme, eg palm trees, a wind-surfer, paddleskis, surf-boards.
2. Have some people from your cell make flower necklaces to put around your guests as they arrive.
3. Organise another cell to help you by serving as waiters and waitresses.
4. Arrange for cell members to perform a few skits or a song or two.

On the evening

1. Have Hawaiian music playing in the background.
2. You can combine a karaoke evening with the Hawaiian theme as a form of entertainment.
3. Have a prize for the person with the most authentic Hawaiian dress.

15 Video evening

This evening also requires very little preparation.

Suggestions

1. Encourage your cell members to invite their friends that they are reaching out to.

2. Make sure that the videos you will be screening are suitable for this type of evening.

3. Ask each cell member to bring along either a packet of crisps, a cool drink or popcorn.

On the evening

1. Prepare a couple of fun ice-breakers. Because of the video, there will not be much talking or socialising, therefore, have the ice-breakers at the beginning to create a fun atmosphere.

16 Outreach picnic

Suggestions

1. Get your cell members to invite their friends.
2. Send out a suggested list of ingredients for the picnic basket to your cell members. Besides the food, you can include items such as plates, cutlery, glasses, a radio, a blanket.
3. Have each person prepare a special little gift to go in the basket (eg a gift-wrapped chocolate) with an inspirational card attached.

Preparation

1. Have single people in the cell prepare a picnic basket for two people. Let couples work together preparing a basket for four people.

On the day

1. Have everybody meet at the venue.
2. As they arrive, take their picnic basket and put it to one side (make a note of how many people each basket caters for).
3. Once everyone has arrived, take a basket and allocate people to it. These people then take their basket and go for a picnic together. (Make sure that nobody gets their own basket.)
4. Avoid pairing off one person from a couple with a single person of the opposite sex.

4
ZONE CELEBRATIONS

Ten tips for zone celebrations

1. Delegation and good organisation are the keys to a successful zone celebration.
2. All the cell leaders and zone supervisors in the particular zone need to work together.
3. Always remember, perfection is law, excellence is grace.
4. Allow enough time for all your cell members to invite their friends, ie three to four weeks.
5. Ensure that the evening is well led — by the person chosen to be master of ceremonies. This is a vital key to the success of the evening.
6. Make sure all visitors are looked after for the entire evening.
7. Use music, decor, props, etc., to create the atmosphere you wish to have.
8. Never pressurise visitors concerning the gospel at these events — allow them to get to know you first, and let your life speak.
9. Welcome visitors publicly.
10. Spend a lot of time praying before the event.

1 Gutter diner

What you need

1. Roof guttering — thoroughly cleaned and disinfected (new if possible).
2. Ice cream — lots of it!
3. Chocolate sauce, nuts, etc.

Lay out the gutter in the middle of the hall and fill it with your choc-nut sundae.

Enjoy an evening of fun, laughter and lots of ice cream at the Gutter Diner. Put up a big sign:

Welcome to the Gutter Diner

2 English tea party

This is an afternoon that is enjoyed by young and old alike.

Dress

English — early twentieth century, or contemporary fashion.

Refreshments

Tea, cucumber sandwiches, scones, cakes, etc.

Activities

Cricket, croquet.

With a little effort this day could be a great success.

3 Barbecue and tennis day

A barbecue is always great, but combine it with a day of social tennis and it becomes a day to remember.

Draw partners for the tennis out of a hat. Mixed doubles works well and it tends to relax any competitiveness.

The barbecue afterwards is always very relaxed as people's inhibitions have been dealt with during the day on the tennis court. It is important to ask everyone to bring a tennis racket and some balls.

Hire a tennis court!

4 Mini golf evening

This is fun event to invite people that the cell is reaching out to. Play in groups of six or more people and enjoy all the laughs. Arrange for the whole group to have hot chocolate afterwards.

5 Inter-zone sports day

Arranging an inter-zone sports day creates the opportunity for all the zones to enjoy a day together.

Possible activities

1. Volley ball
2. Football
3. Tug-o-war
4. Baseball
5. Relay races.

Organise refreshments for the day and hot dogs and hamburgers for lunch.

6 Formal top/casual bottom party

This evening is arranged as a zone outreach dinner party.

The theme, as it suggests, insists that everyone wears something formal above the waist (eg top hat and tails) and something really casual below the waist (eg beach shorts and sandals).

The entire evening is the dinner party. Skits, songs and jokes can be arranged beforehand to create an atmosphere in between the courses of the meal.

This type of evening takes a lot of organisation, but it is well worth the effort.

7 Medieval banquet

This event takes a bit of planning beforehand, but the success of the evening will be well worth it.

The banquet hall

To add to the authenticity of the evening, we suggest decorating the hall in medieval style. This can be accomplished by covering the walls with black plastic bags or something similar. Once this has been done, ask some creative people to paint pictures such as shields, swords, horses, etc., on the covering. The tables can be decorated with ivy and the refreshments, such as potato crisps and peanuts, are just put straight onto the table cloths — the evening is very primitive. A good idea for plates for the main meal is to cut a log of wood into 'plates' of 20 mm thickness.

Each person at the banquet would have a specific role to play and would have to be dressed appropriately. For example, the king and queen would be the zone supervisor and his wife, the lords and ladies would be the cell leaders and the cell members would be the servants. On arriving the cell members are given their dress for the evening, which is a black plastic bag. They have to make holes for their arms and head. Other characters you can have are two wenches (per table, they will do the serving), a jester who plays jokes on everyone, and guards.

There are a number of rules that need to be adhered to by all. These rules need to be explained to the group at the beginning of the evening. No one may enter the hall until they have heard the rules. Have everybody congregate outside the banquet hall and read the following rules to them:

1. Have a human statue painted in gold at the entrance. When entering the medieval banquet hall, each person is to stop, look up at the statue and repeat the following: 'How regal that dost seem to me, with eyes so wild and face so free, bid me enter at squire's call, into this medieval banquet hall'. If you fail to recite the rhyme correctly, punishment will be rendered at a later stage.
2. Servants are to call their cell leaders 'lord' and 'lady' at all times, and may only use a cell leader's surname, eg Lady Edwards.
3. Servants may do nothing without their master's permission.
4. The words cold drink may not be mentioned. The word to use is MEAD.
5. Should anybody require salt, permission to fetch it from the royal table must be sought from your lord and lady.
6. To fetch salt the servant must come bowed to the royal table and remain bowed in silence until they are acknowledged by the king. They then respond: 'Sire, I require salt for my squire!'

7. The lord and lady may eat at any time. The servants may only eat when the king is seated.
8. Everybody, except those at the royal table, may only eat with their left hand.
9. Permission to go to the toilet must be sought from your lord or lady.
10. The word toilet may not be used. Instead you have to say the following:
    Men: 'May I point Percy at the porcelain?'
    Ladies: 'May I take Alice to the chalice?'
11. Any rule disobeyed, broken or ignored is punishable in the stocks.
12. The king has the liberty and authority to institute new rules at will.

Here is an example of a typical invitation for the night:

Medieval Banquet

Date: 18 September 1999
Time: 7 pm

Venue: St Peter's Church Hall, High Street

Cost: £10 person

Admit One

---

8 Fashion show evening

This event involves arranging a fun fashion show, using members from your zone as the models. The women and men model clothes, either their own or from a store, in different categories, eg summer wear, winter wear, sports outfits, formal evening wear.

A wonderful show-stopper is the wedding dress section, where women model their own wedding dresses.

A 'cheese and wine' evening can be organised to round off what promises to be a night to remember.

9 Airport party

You can really go to town with this evening in making it as real as possible with aeroplane sounds, air hostesses, etc.

Planning

Each cell in the zone is requested to select a country which they wish to represent on the evening, in terms of clothing, decorating and food. They also have to prepare a three-minute presentation on that country,

A section of the hall must be cordoned off and will be made to look like the inside of an aeroplane. The other section of the hall is divided into however many cells are representing countries. This section has to be decorated in the style of the country being represented. For example, if the country is Hawaii, they would decorate their section with

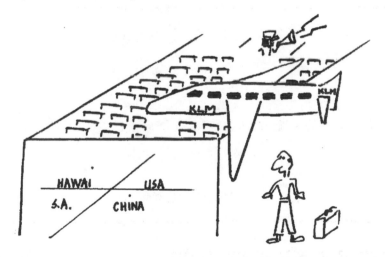

parasols, surf-boards, grass skirts, etc. Each cell will be allocated a course of the meal, either the starter, main meal, dessert or coffee. This has to co-ordinate with the country that they are representing. It must be a traditional meal, eg if they were representing Italy and they had the main meal to prepare, they could possibly prepare Lasagne. After each meal, the captain would announce the departure of the flight to its following destination. All the passengers would then move back to their seats on the aeroplane.

On the aeroplane side, seats are arranged to represent those in an aeroplane. The events on the aeroplane should simulate what happens on a genuine flight, eg emergency flight procedures must be acted out by air hostesses, drinks can be served from trolleys, aeroplane sounds can be recreated. You can even go as far as recreating a hi-jacking or a crash landing where your emergency gear could be used.

During the flight, a member from the cell representing the country that they are flying to, would give a short presentation on the history, traditions and climatic conditions pertaining to that country. Meanwhile, the rest of the cell would be preparing the meal in the other section of the hall. Ice-breakers can also be made use of during the simulated flight, but, these ice breakers need to be of such a nature that the guests remain seated.

Bon voyage!

5
CELL CAMPS

Ten tips for cell camps

1. It is important to plan fun activities for the duration of the camp. These activities must be designed for relationship and team building.

2. Divide your camp into 'flock groups' for more intimate ministry and practical events such as kitchen duty, sports, etc.

3. Leave enough time for ministry and sharing as this is part of the purpose of a cell camp.

4. Do not over-structure the camp — be flexible.

5. Decide on the purpose of the camp first and then plan your events around your purpose.

6. Use the element of surprise to make the camp more exciting.

7. Immerse your camp in prayer, trusting the Lord for breakthroughs in the lives of your cell members.

8. Be creative with your cell camp invitation as this will draw people or turn them away.

9. Choose your venue carefully — it is always good to inspect a number of venues before choosing one.

10. All that you do must foster the feeling of community living. Avoid serious competition that could become negative.

1 Bridge-building competition

You require the following for each team

1. Fifty tongue depressors (available at your local chemist)
2. One roll of Sellotape
3. Two metres of string
4. Two sheets of A4 paper

Divide your cell into teams of about five. Each team has exactly one hour to use the materials provided to build a bridge. It may not be shorter than 25 centimetres or narrower than 15 centimetres.

After an hour each bridge is given a mark for:
1. Strength — test it by placing bricks on the bridge until it breaks.
2. Aesthetics — check to see how ingenious the designs are.
3. Teamwork — evaluate them while they are working. Watch for people not participating or those that are taking over.

2 Photo race

This is a great activity for a cell camp. The cell members are divided into groups (four to five in a group).

Each group needs:
1. Twenty-four exposure film
2. Camera
3. All the relevant cryptic clues
4. Car.

Each group is given approximately two hours to accomplish this task.

They must decipher all the cryptic clues and then go to the place that each clue reveals. At this place someone needs to take a photograph of the whole group to prove that they were there.

The group must then go to a one-hour photo shop and persuade them to develop the photos quickly. The first group home with all the correct photographs wins the prize.

3 Stalk the lantern

This old favourite is enjoyed by all on any cell camp.

What you need

1. Gas lantern
2. Small flag on a stick
3. Elastic bands (enough for each person)
4. Torches for the leaders

This activity works best late at night. Each person is given an elastic band to wear around their wrist. (This signifies their

life and they may only continue playing the game as long as they keep their elastic band.)

The purpose of the activity is to locate the lantern (hidden somewhere in the field or wood), stalk up to it and attempt to grab the flag (placed next to the lantern).

The leaders are prowling around with torches trying to catch any unsuspecting cell members.

If one is physically caught, their elastic band is removed and they return to the camp to wait for the end of the game.

This activity also works well in teams of men against women.

4 Four-way soccer

This is a fun activity that is a little crazy. Normal rules of soccer apply except that there are four teams playing with one ball.

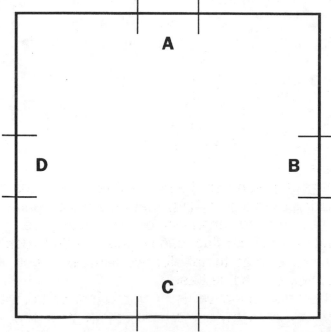

Team A scores in team C's goal and team C scores in team A's goal. Team B scores in team D's goal and team D scores in team B's goal.

To add even more fun, play this game early in the morning before sunrise or at dusk.

5 War games

This game works well with camps consisting of a large number of people. Divide the group up into four teams of approximately eight people in a team. The teams are each given a different coloured flag on a stick — that becomes the team flag.

This game is played in an open area and each team is instructed to create a home base of two metres by two metres, comprised of stones on the ground. The flag is erected in the centre of the home base. The home bases are all in different locations of the open area.

The object of the game is to steal one another's flags. The team with their flag stolen is immediately disqualified. The team members therefore have to organise themselves into 'defenders' and 'attackers'. The defenders stand around the flag within their home base, protecting it and the attackers go out to attempt to steal the other team's flags. A person on the defence team defends their flag by attempting to touch anybody that enters their home base. As soon as somebody enters an enemy home base attempting to steal the flag, should you, the defender, touch them, they have to go to 'jail' for two minutes. (Their 'jail' would be their own home base.)

The attackers' objective, is to create a diversion with the defenders at the enemy home base, allowing for one of the attackers' team members to dart into the enemy home base and steal the flag. As soon as a team's flag has been removed, that team retreats to the hall or tent and waits for the game to end. The game ends when one team has got all the flags.

6 Mini olympics

This is good for an afternoon activity. It can be arranged with all the fanfare of a major olympics. Teams can choose a theme song for their entrance parade.

Have the teams sit next to one another around the mini-sports field, with all the activities revolving around sport, but in a mini fashion. For example, instead of throwing javelin, they would see who could throw a straw the farthest or have shot-put with a ping-pong ball, etc.

The whole afternoon would be based around points scored at the various activities. The winning team would then be the team with the most points.

To create a more festive atmosphere, have music playing in the background and encourage the teams to cheer on their team members with war cries.

7 Faith, hope and love

The group is divided into three teams. Each team is given a theme — either faith, hope or love. The team is taken into an area around the campsite and has to depict an abstract scene of either faith, hope or love using only natural materials.

Each team is allocated an hour to organise their presentation. The team with the best depiction at the end wins.

8 Flags

This activity is best for a younger cell and if the camp is taking place at the coast.

Everybody lies stomach down facing away from sticks which are placed in the ground approximately fifty metres away. There is one stick fewer than the number of people participating.

At the sound of the whistle, the contestants have to jump

up and run to grab a stick. Whoever doesn't get a stick is disqualified. The number of sticks is reduced by one after each run. This continues until such time as you are left with two people who have to dash to grab the last stick. The winner is the person who grabs the last stick.

9 Animal hunt

This is very similar to stalk the lantern. It also takes place at night. A large bushy area is cordoned off. The camp participants are left in the hall or tent while the leaders hide within a cordoned-off area. The leaders are each given a certain number of bands on which is written the name of an animal (each leader is allocated a different animal name). The campers in the hall or tent are informed that they have to go out in teams and hunt down the animals. Once a leader has been found, the team then removes one of his armbands. The leader then goes back into hiding.

Beforehand, the leaders allocate points per animal. At the end of the game, the winning team would be the one with the most points, not necessarily the most armbands.

10 Blob

The men and women are divided up into two teams. The men have to organise themselves into a big 'blob' on the ground and knot themselves up by grabbing onto each other. The women have to discuss how they are going to get the men apart — no tickling, scratching, etc, is allowed. On the word 'Go', the women have to attempt to separate the men in the shortest time possible. Once they have separated all the men, the women then organise themselves into a knotted blob and the men attempt to part them in a shorter time period than the women.

It is best to work together in smaller teams when attempting the separation.

11 Cell camp bonfire

Everybody is divided into groups of approximately four or five people. They then spend an hour or two preparing a skit which they have to present at the cell camp bonfire.

Later in the evening when it is dark, everybody gets together around the bonfire where they sing songs and hymns. Each team then does a presentation of their funny skit, drama, song or something that will make the bonfire more enjoyable.

This activity is wonderful for giving testimonies, etc.

12 Lead the blind

Usually used on the first evening of a camp to teach people the need to rely on one another.

Divide the group into teams of approximately six or seven.

Every person in the team is blindfolded, except the leader of each team. The team are then taken on an obstacle course around the campsite with only the leader shouting out orders concerning the terrain. They need to listen without seeing and respond to the leader's voice while going through ditches, over small poles, etc. This teaches the team dependency.

When the teams get back, you can have a discussion regarding 'becoming dependent, trusting and relying on your brothers and sisters in Christ'.

6
SOLUTIONS

Fun ice-breakers

5 Missing words
One day on the Isle of **Wight** — it was **light** that **night** if I recall — I was standing looking out over the **bight** when I saw a terrible **sight**. Billy and Bertha were having a **fight**.

Bertha had said, 'Billy, you're **tight**!'

And Billy replied with a slur, 'Bertha, you know, you just **might** be **right**!'

6 African adventure
See page 134

20 Cell IQ test
1. Blood is thicker than water
2. High above the clouds
3. Overwhelming odds
4. Line up
5. You ought to be in pictures
6. Put it in writing
7. You're under arrest
8. Mixed doubles tennis
9. Just in case
10. Ill in bed
11. Getting it all together
12. Tea for two
13. Call it a day
14. No U turn
15. Endless love

54 General knowledge quiz
1. The Angel Falls
2. Jupiter
3. Yellow (it is a gemstone)
4. It is about to leave port
5. Five
6. Leonardo de Vinci
7. Corgies
8. England and Australia
9. Indigo
10. Roubles
11. It is your kneecap
12. A barometer
13. Twenty-four
14. South Africa
15. Canberra
16. Haggai
17. South Africa
18. Calgary, Canada
19. Weight
20. A word that reads the same spelt backwards or forwards (eg madam)

55 True or false
1. False — Istanbul and Paris
2. True
3. False — Sulphur
4. False — National Aeronautics Space Administration
5. True
6. True
7. False — ferrets can catch human colds
8. True
9. False — Solomon did
10. False — on the moon
11. True
12. True
13. False — entirely cholesterol free
14. True
15. False — Japan

16. True
17. False — six
18. False — Noah was
19. True
20. John — the beloved disciple

57 Capital question

1. Algiers
2. Brussels
3. Ottawa
4. Copenhagen
5. Mogadishu
6. Warsaw
7. Cardiff
8. Beirut
9. Lilongwe
10. Lagos
11. Madrid
12. Canberra
13. Kampala
14. Caracas
15. Ankara
16. Aden
17. Sophia
18. Bucharest
19. Amman
20. Budapest

6 African adventure

7
INDEX

Fun ice-breakers

Serious ice-breakers

Cell outreach events

Zone celebrations

Cell camps

BODY
&Cell

Making the transition to CELL CHURCH: a first-hand account

'In July, we scrapped our house groups. In October we began meeting in cell groups. We did not realise what a revolutionary step we were taking...' So begins Howard Astin's account of his church's transformation from a caring but inward-looking parish to a Christian community where every member really counts.

- ■ **Foreword by Lawrence Singlehurst,**
  Director YWAM, England

- ■ ***Illustrates cell church principles through a local church becoming a real community***

- ■ ***How to create points of entry for visitors***

- ■ ***Includes Pastoral care; teaching courses; lay training; nurture of new members and much more***

The Rev. Howard Astin has been a minister at St John's, Bowling, Bradford, since 1988.

Body & Cell
Howard Astin
ISBN 1 85424 409 4

Available from your local Christian Bookshop.
In case of difficulty contact Monarch Books,
Concorde House, Grenville Place, Mill Hill, London NW7 3SA

MONARCH
BOOKS